Destination Happiness

A WORKBOOK BY

LISSA PATTERSON

Destination Happiness

A Faith Based Approach to Regaining Power Over Addictions and Destructive Behaviors

Brought to you by Metanoia Life Recovery Coaching

For more information, email Lissa at metanoialrc@gmail.com

ISBN: 979-8-9956266-0-2 (Paperback)
ISBN: 979-8-9956266-1-9 (Ebook)

Cover Design by The Royal Writers
Interior Design by The Royal Writers

Dedication

This book is dedicated to you. My brother or sister, fighting to regain his or her power over addictions and destructive behaviors. The person that has it inside of them to win this war against the actions they are currently or have previously committed and live a happy, healthy life. A life full of the kind of joy that can only be found in Jesus Christ.

It's not a coincidence this book is in your hands at this moment. God has a way of placing things exactly where they need to be at the exact time someone needs them. He knows you completely. Your needs and desires. He knows you need help now and has placed this book in front of you so that you may live.

This book is also dedicated to our Father. I am so grateful to Him for leading me out of my personal version of hell. I had already proven to myself that I could not leave on my own and once I relinquished control to Him, my detestable life became a life worth living. Without Him, His love, mercy and grace, my life is meaningless. He wants happiness for you too and has given you the opportunity to learn the very things He taught me along the way. Thank you Father!

> *24 Now all glory to God, who is able to keep you from falling away and will bring you with great joy into his glorious presence without a single fault. 25 All glory to him who alone is God, our Savior through Jesus Christ our Lord. All glory, majesty, power, and authority are his before all time, and in the present, and beyond all time! Amen. (Jude 24-25 NLT)*

Put your words in writing and teach others. Love them through their addictions, heal their minds from abuse and teach them to love themselves. I heard it loud and clear but chose to ignore Him for over a year. I began to hear it more frequently and I argued. Why me? I'm not qualified. I'm not competent. "I have given you the experience and the tools, child. Write. I will guide your hand." was the reply.

> *Have I not commanded you? Be strong and courageous. Do not be afraid; do not be discouraged, for the Lord your God will be with you wherever you go." (Joshua 1:9, NIV)*

Contents

Preface

Hi. My name is Lissa, and I used to be an alcoholic. At the time of publication, it has been over 9 years since I had my last sip.

The story of my life is one that used to be difficult for me to tell. It contains chapter upon chapter of abuse, grief and turmoil. Alcohol spilled across the pages through the years. Tiny drops to begin with. Just when I needed to feel like I fit in or let my guard down a little bit. Mostly to loosen up and become somebody that normally wasn't. Someone more fun and likable. Less inhibited. Anybody other than who I believed myself to be.

I grew to hate myself more as my story unfolded. The tiny drops expanded like paint splatters covering the words on each page, until eventually, the pages were almost completely covered. I had become an every night drinker. Not merely a drink or two. I lived for the time I could sit with the bottle, trying to forget who I was. Attempting to drown out memories and misery. The entire book of my life reeked of alcohol, desperation and despair.

Inside the margins of my book was my walk with God. That's exactly what I would describe it as too. Marginal. When I was young, my sisters and I attended church with our mother. I remember disliking church. While pounding on the pulpit, the preacher aggressively lectured about sin and how anyone that sinned would go to hell. He taught that God was angered by sinners. And because of the abuse I was living through, I thought I must be a sister of Satan. Church was the place where I was reminded of my powerlessness, unworthiness and shame. That's how I felt anyway. Lower than the dirt underneath your shoes.

During my childhood, I was convinced that God couldn't and didn't love me. I was a bad girl. I was a sinner. I was unlovable. I prayed and wept and cried out to Him, but all I heard was silence. I didn't understand how He could let horrible things happen to children or why I was chosen to live in hell. I felt He had abandoned me, and I became angry. So angry that I turned my back to Him. If He didn't care about me, then I didn't care about Him. I held this grudge for many years, through each of my horrendous relationships, and into my mid-forties.

As I continued to tolerate my life, going through the motions of living and drinking myself into oblivion, it became very obvious to me that what I was doing wasn't working. I needed help in a big way and only our big Father in Heaven would be able to provide what I needed. I found myself literally on my knees, sobbing uncontrollably, begging Him to love me enough to give me the strength to stop drinking and live a life that would please Him. A life that I could be happy with. Since we're being honest and vulnerable here, I'll tell you that I didn't think He was listening. I assumed that so many years of staring at the back of my head, listening to me curse Him had hardened His heart towards me. I thought He had deemed me unworthy and written me out of His will. One night, I allowed my mind to be quiet enough to hear "I have given you the tools because I love you child. You just need to use them." Praise God! Hallelujah! I may have given up on myself, but He hadn't.

Soon after that night, I drove by the store where I used to stop for a bottle, smiling while I said a prayer of thanks, and kept driving towards home. Ten months later, I was given the courage to leave an extremely abusive, codependent relationship. Today, I've never felt stronger or more empowered.

God covered the alcohol stains before this chapter of my life in Jesus' blood and I'm so thankful that He gave me clean pages to write on from here to eternity. Just so you know, I'm not getting any special treatment. He loves you every bit as much as He loves me.

> *In his kindness God called you to share in his eternal glory by means of Christ Jesus. So after you have suffered a little while, he will restore, support, and strengthen you, and he will place you on a firm foundation. (1 Peter 5:10, NLT)*

Approximately five years ago, I was contemplating the writing I had been told to put on paper while scrolling through Facebook. I noticed an advertisement for Life Coach Training. Something inside me (I'm sure it was the Holy Spirit) said, "This is useful" After many hours, days, weeks and months of studying, I obtained more knowledge than I ever thought possible as well as the following certifications:

Master Mindset Life Coach

Emotional Intelligence (EQ) Life Coach

Confidence Life Coach

Happiness Life Coach

Cognitive Behavioral (CBT) Life Coach

Rational Emotive Behavior Therapy (REBT) Life Coach

Life Purpose Coach

Goal success Life Coach

Professional Life Coach

Neurolinguistics Programming (NLP) Practitioner

However, I was still not confident in my task. I had an overwhelming desire to start writing but couldn't decide how to start or what to write. I doubted that I had enough knowledge to be helpful to others. I feared that I wouldn't get it right or would fail. It was after much debate that He put another training in front of me. Life Coach Ministry. Not only was I able to complete courses to become a Life Coach Minister, I became Ordained. If someone had told me I would be on this path before our Father spoke to me, I would have either laughed until I hurt or hurt the person saying it.

I struggled with finding the time to accomplish the project ahead of me. I soon realized that not only was I not confident with myself, but I was also lacking faith that God would provide as He has promised many times in His own writing. But again, He did. I gently placed my worries in the palms of His hands, and He gifted me with an opportunity that would allow me to do as He had asked. He is so good to me!

I've spent most of my life asking the Heavens why I am here on earth. What is my purpose? It is clear to me now that He was preparing me to utilize the gifts He has bestowed upon me. To serve Him and my brothers and sisters. One woman, given the opportunity to help hundreds of thousands of other people to heal. I pray that after you find peace, you will use your God given gifts to serve Him and others as well.

Acknowledgements

God knows us better than we know ourselves. Before we were even conceived, he knew us. He knew what we would look like, what our personalities would be, what struggles we would face, what we would desire. And he knew exactly what people we would need to shape us as well as support us. He knew we would need a few extra special people in our lives and chose those people specifically for us. I have been blessed with the best of the best.

Alissa, my precious daughter. I'm so sorry for creating a life that was as unpleasant for you as it was for me. I pray daily that you continue to heal from the behaviors of the addicted person I used to be. You unknowingly provided me with inspiration to write so that other children and their parents may be liberated from similar adversity. Thank you for supporting my crazy ideas (like writing this book) and giving me reason to not give up. Jesus and I both love you more than I could possibly put into words.

Stefanie and Telina, my sisters in Christ and by blood. The two of you are my rocks. You have both remained steadily by my side when my days were dark and I couldn't gather enough courage or strength to even wipe my tears. For years you endured drunken crying late night phone calls along with constant grumbling about my unhappiness with life. During my time of need, not only were you there for me, but you continuously reminded me that God was with me and wanted to help. Without your encouragement and support, I don't know that I would have found my way back to Him. Thank you for continuing to listen to me through the time of writing and editing when all I could think or talk about was getting the words out of my heart and into the hands of those that needed them. There aren't enough words to express my gratitude and love for you.

Beta Readers, my family of Christ Followers. Thank you for volunteering your time to read through my writing and provide feedback. Your encouragement, support and advice served as confirmation that I was indeed called to write it and that although it needed a few minor changes, it is exactly what somebody needs to begin their own journey back to God and a life void of addiction and full of joy.

Mr. Wright for reminding me every Sunday morning that someone needed this book and gently nudged me to bring it to completion as an act of obedience. Without your kind words, this writing may be still gathering dust on my desk.

Debbie Love, my good friend and sister in Christ. Thank you so much for taking the time and effort to guide me through punctuation and grammatical edits. The encouragement and brilliant insights you scattered throughout the pages are invaluable.

Dear Heavenly Father,

I humbly come to you today to ask you to deafen Satan's ears and mind to my thoughts as I travel towards a life that is free of self destruction. I pray that you help me to keep an open mind to the things I am learning and help me understand. I know Father, that you created me to lead a better life than I currently have and that my past is meant to guide me towards growth. Although I didn't see it before, you have been beside me throughout my entire life. You have watched me stumble and fall, just waiting for me to ask for your help. Today, I am asking that it be your will for me to be free of all addictions and destructive behaviors. I need supernatural help and healing that only you can provide Father, and I need it now. Please provide me with Your grace, strength and courage as I move into the unknown. In Jesus name I pray, Amen.

Chapter 1

Pre-Trip Inspection and Planning

Here we are. You and me. We're embarking on a new adventure to a destination that may seem thousands of miles away or may appear to be just over the horizon. There may be sharp curves and steep slopes, or the road could be so straight that you can see for miles ahead. Either way, we are in this together. God is in the pace car. You are not alone.

Before we put the car in drive, let's talk about our journey. During the course of our travels, I want you to remember this: This book isn't going to fix you. You aren't broken. You are simply a person that has made decisions in life that you are about to put in the rear-view mirror.

To get a clear picture of our destination, let me ask you this. Who would you be if the role of "addict" were to disappear tomorrow? You wake up in the morning and no longer use, drink, gamble, whatever your poison is - who are you? What kind of person do you want to be? How would your behaviors be different? In what ways will your ethics and morals change? Think about it, imagine it and hold on to your answer.

Did you notice I said "role of addict?" This is because "addict" is not WHO you are. "Addict" is a role you have played in your life. You may play the role of teacher, lawyer or mechanic today, but that role may change and you place yourself in the role of doctor or racecar driver. Someone that struggles with anxiety isn't anxiety. A person that suffers from cancer isn't cancer. And someone that has an addiction isn't addiction. You see? These things aren't WHO you are. They're titles given to you according to what you do or a state you're in. We'll talk more about this later.

You're not completely happy with your life as it is now, you're simply tolerating what is now your "normal".

I also want to point out that there will be times in our travels when you want to resist. You'll want to slam on the brakes and not move another inch forward. Please understand that this is not unusual. Our brains sometimes resist change because we fear the unknown. When you feel this urge, remember the reason that you want to change is because there is something in your life you're discontent with. You're not completely happy with your life as it is now, you're simply tolerating what is now your "normal". It's okay to rest for a minute. While you're resting, lay the seat back and think about your answer to the "who do you want to be" question.

> *Watch and pray so that you will not fall into temptation. The spirit is willing, but the flesh is weak. (Mark 14:38, NIV)*

I want to point out that God didn't create you to live a life of pain and misery. He wants you to breathe love, live love and be love. His plan is for you to be joyful. He wants your life to be spectacular. God says you are a lot more than you think. If you are a believer and have accepted Jesus Christ as your savior, He says:

You are God's child.

> *But to all who believed him and accepted him, he gave the right to become children of God. (John 1:12, NLT)*

You are a friend of Jesus.

> *I no longer call you servants, because a servant does not know his master's business. Instead, I have called you friends, for everything that I learned from my Father I have made known to you. (John 15:15, NIV)*

You are Christ's family.

> *All of you together are Christ's body, and each of you is a part of it. (1 Corinthians 12:27, NLT)*

You are complete.

> *So you also are complete through your union with Christ, who is the head over every ruler and authority. (Colossians 2:10, NLT)*

You are a citizen of Heaven.

> *But we are citizens of heaven, where the Lord Jesus Christ lives. And we are eagerly waiting for him to return as our Savior. (Philippians 3:20, NLT)*

You are God's masterpiece.

> *For we are God's masterpiece. He has created us anew in Christ Jesus, so we can do the good things he planned for us long ago. (Ephesians 2:10, NLT)*

The Holy Spirit doesn't leave you just because you're behaving less than perfectly.

You might be thinking that these things don't apply to you because of things you've done, words you've said, or choices that you've made. You're wrong though. Just like I was wrong when I assumed He had written me off. If at any time you accepted Jesus into your heart, He sent the Holy Spirit to dwell within you. The Holy Spirit doesn't leave you just because you're behaving less than perfectly. Call on and listen to Him, and He will give you wisdom and knowledge in every situation. He will help you to make better decisions. It's your choice whether you pay attention to His guidance or ignore His instructions for overcoming and reaching your Destination Happiness. I know you'll make the right choice.

If you haven't accepted Jesus Christ into your heart yet, my prayer is that you open your heart to Him. You too can experience the wonderful love that only He can give. Our Father already loves you tremendously. You don't even have to earn it. All you need to do is accept Him. I encourage you to keep reading.

> *1 Out of the stump of David's family will grow a shoot—yes, a new Branch bearing fruit from the old root. 2 And the Spirit of the Lord will rest on him—the Spirit of wisdom and understanding, the Spirit of counsel and might, the Spirit of knowledge and the fear of the Lord. (Isaiah 11:1-2, NLT)*

God's plans for you and your life are beyond your imagination.

> *"For I know the plans I have for you," says the Lord. "They are plans for good and not for disaster, to give you a future and a hope." (Jeremiah 29:11, NLT)*

God gives you instructions for living a meaningful life. You'll find a lot of these instructions scattered throughout this book. His wisdom is found in every chapter and should be scattered throughout your heart in everything you do as well.

> *15–16 So be very careful how you live, not being like those with no understanding, but live honorably with true wisdom, for we are living in evil times. Take full advantage of every day as you spend your life for his purposes. 17 And don't live foolishly for then you will have discernment to fully understand God's will. 18 And don't get drunk with wine, which is rebellion; instead be filled continually with the Holy Spirit. 19 And your hearts will overflow with a joyful song to the Lord. Keep speaking to each other with words of Scripture, singing the Psalms with praises and spontaneous songs given by the Spirit! 20 Always give thanks to Father God for every person he brings into your life in the name of our Lord Jesus Christ. (Ephesians 5:15-20, TPT)*

> *No, O people, the Lord has told you what is good, and this is what he requires of you: to do what is right, to love mercy, and to walk humbly with your God. (Micah 6:8, NLT)*

Set Out With a Vision

Earlier, I asked you to think about what your life will be like once you have kicked your addiction to the curb. On the next few pages, you're going to have the opportunity to create a vision for your future. This vision is where your journey is going to take you. Your "Destination Happiness". You're going to answer a series of questions. Once you have given each question thought and have answers to each, you'll assemble them into story format to compose a movie that you can replay in your mind. In your story, it helps to add specific descriptions such as what you smell, what you're wearing, who is in the movie with you, what you're doing, etc. It is very important to leave out details that remind you of anything negative, using your poison of choice, and so on. Another note is that you may not use the answer to every question in your picture and movie, however it helps to have these things in your mind so that subconsciously you know the details for more vivid visualization and so that your brain doesn't have to question them.

Do you want to hear something crazy? Good! I was planning to tell you anyway. Studies have shown that you can sit or lay around and visualize doing an activity on a regular basis and actually improve your strength, endurance and performance of that activity just by visualizing that you're doing it. Yep. That's right. Your thoughts are so powerful that regularly sitting in your recliner visualizing yourself exercising can significantly increase your strength without you even moving. If your brain can do that, imagine how it can be used to stop your addictive behaviors! What you imagine yourself experiencing can create a real outcome in your life. Which is why this vision exercise is so important. Once you've completed this activity, it's vital to take a few minutes everyday to visualize it. Ready? I'm so excited!

Before getting started, think about these four things. 1) When are you most the person you want to be? 2) What are you doing during these times? 3) What are your dreams? 4) What do you really want? Write your vision as if you've already accomplished your goals, knowing that whatever it is that you desire can be learned and you can improve anything in order to get there.

As you progress through your recovery, your vision will change. As you become "sober" your thought processes become more positive and as you begin to realize that you are more capable than you have given yourself credit for, you will drive yourself towards higher goals.

If you're not a verbally creative person, putting it all together can be challenging so I have included a short version of one of my life visions as an example for you. Yes, I said "one of". I have several dreams that have the same base principals (such as career), but different places and things. It isn't a bad idea to create more than one for yourself. In the future when you're playing your movie, you may not feel like being at the beach at that moment and would rather envision relaxing in front of your fireplace or being surrounded by family on Christmas morning. It's your vision. Create whatever you want.

Create Your Vision Worksheet

When I think about my happy place, where am I? ______

What time of year do I want to be here? ______

Where in my happy place am I? ______

What am I doing? ______

What am I wearing? (Be descriptive) ______

______

______

How does the temperature feel? ______

______

______

What things do I see in my happy place? Describe each item. (If outdoors, what is the landscape? If indoors, what items are in the room?) ______

______

______

______

______

______

What scents do I smell? Describe the scents and what is creating them. ______

______

______

______

What sounds do I hear, where are they coming from, and what is making them? __________

____

____

____

____

____

____

Who is with me? Where is their location? What are they doing? What are they wearing? (Skip this question if you are alone or use additional paper if needed. If you have not yet met the characters you desire to be included in your vision, imagine who they would be and what they look like.)

Person 1? ______________________________

Location? ______________________________

Doing? ______________________________

Wearing? ______________________________

Person 2? ______________________________

Location? ______________________________

Doing? ______________________________

Wearing? ______________________________

Person 3? ______________________________

Location? ______________________________

Doing? ______________________________

Wearing? ______________________________

Person 4? ____________________

Location? ____________________

Doing? ____________________

Wearing? ____________________

Person 5? ____________________

Location? ____________________

Doing? ____________________

Wearing? ____________________

Other descriptions such as if you're eating, what are you eating? What does it look like? What does it taste like? Etc. What do things feel like when touched? ____________________

____

____

What emotions am I feeling while in this location, with these people, doing these things?

____

____

What is my dream job and why? ____________________

____

What kind of car did I drive to my happy place? (Describe vehicle) ____________________

____

____

What are some things I am thankful for? ____________________

____

____

Putting Your Vision into a Picture Worksheet

Example Vision

I am relaxing on white sand at Coco Beach as my daughter, her husband and my granddaughter are playing in the ocean. I feel the warmth of the sunshine kissing my skin and a slight cool breeze blowing through my hair. The sky is the most beautiful shade of blue I have ever seen and there are tourists on various colors of beach towels scattered all over the sand several yards away.

As I deeply inhale the clean yet salty air, I feel gratitude that I am able to afford a family vacation with income from writing books and coaching others towards living their best life. I know that I am helping them get to a place in their own lives where they can comfortably take a vacation too.

My thoughts are interrupted by the sounds of laughter and waves. I look out to see my granddaughter attempting to dunk her dad into the water as another wave approaches. My daughter is giggling at the same sight. I love the sound of them laughing. My heart is full. I thank my Father above for blessing me with grace and mercy as well as the opportunities He has presented to me.

Roll it!

I hope you had a lot of feel good moments when creating your vision. For me, putting it together elicited feelings of peace, love and excitement all at once.

Now it's time for the good stuff! This is where you'll use a lot of the details from the questionnaire. Use your answers in the following imagination exercise.

Find a quiet place where you can relax for a few minutes without distractions. It can be anywhere you can get away for a little bit. I once had a mother tell me that when she first started playing her movie, she would tell her family she was taking a shower and hid in her master bath because it was the only place she knew she wouldn't be interrupted. Now, follow me here:

1. Sit, lay, whatever, in a position that will be comfortable through the duration of this exercise.
2. Once you're comfortable, close your eyes and start to focus on your breathing. Feel the air entering your nose and lungs, then exiting your nose and lungs. Notice your

body relaxing. Notice how the air feels as it enters your nostrils. Is it warm? Cool? Take a minute to notice how it smells.

3. Imagine that you're looking at the air from its source all the way to your nostrils. watching it waft from beginning all the way to your lungs. Take a minute to notice how it looks entering your nostrils, then exiting. Notice how it smells.
4. Exhale a long, slow breath. During this exhale, imagine the air leaving your nostrils and expanding. It is now opening up into your entire field of vision. When it clears, you see a picture of your happy place. Take a minute to look around from your location. Notice the items in your picture.
5. See the people in your picture one at a time. Notice where in your picture each of them are located. Notice what each appears to be doing. Notice what they are wearing. Notice the expressions on each face.
6. Now imagine the entire picture. The people and things in your happy place all come together from where you are located. Take a minute to look around. Notice how you feel emotionally in this moment.
7. Still focusing on your picture, begin to imagine sounds in the background. Remember the smell in the air.
8. Now imagine the items that should have motion are functioning. Allow the people in your picture to move around. doing whatever your imagination wants them to do.
9. Notice your movie. Notice how you feel emotionally in this moment. Keep it in your mind for as long as possible.

It may help to memorize the steps before you try to visualize so that you don't have to distract yourself to either try to remember or read them again. If they are still a bit difficult to remember, ask someone you trust to read them to you, in a calm voice, or record yourself, putting at least 15 seconds between each one. The more you practice this exercise, the easier it will be for you to remember the steps.

Keeping your vision in motion for more than a few seconds may be difficult at first. I'm not an imaginative person so when I first began practicing imagery, I would replay the same two or three second clip over and over until I was able to expand it. Now I can have conversations with the people in my movie. It's like selective daydreaming. The important things are that you can see what your vision looks like and feel how you imagine you would feel during your movie.

Chapter 2

Driving on Flat Tires - Your Addiction

One thing almost every addicted person has in common is that they spend a great deal of time denying that they have an addiction. If you're honest with yourself, you'll realize that at one time (and maybe still) you had convinced yourself that indulging in your poison was merely an insignificant habit that you could quit any time you chose. Yet when you tried to stop the behavior, you found it to be more difficult than you thought.

Addiction can be defined as repeatedly engaging in behaviors or using substances regardless of the outcome and consequences. This can be compulsive, chronic, physiological or psychological. Something tells you that you need your poison of choice even if you know it's causing harm or you are trying to free yourself from it.

Fact is, almost every person in America and around the globe is addicted to something.

One common misconception about people with addictions is that they are "bad" people. The fact is, almost every person in America and around the globe is addicted to something. It may be meth, heroin, pills, alcohol, sex, adrenaline, sugar, love, acceptance, caffeine, food, gaming, shopping, gambling, social media or even cell phones. Does that mean that almost every person around the world is a "bad" person? I think not! Some addicts may exhibit additional destructive behaviors which are considered "bad," but they themselves are not "bad" just because they are addicted to something. They are nothing more than people that continuously indulge in less than desirable habits.

Look at the people around you. The loan officer sitting at a desk in the bank may be addicted. The woman in front of you in the checkout line may be addicted. The well-dressed man sitting in the pew beside you at church may be addicted. Your boss or coworker may be addicted. Even your state Governor may be living with some kind of addiction. Addiction can get a firm grip on anybody at any time. It's a common condition in America although we may not be able to pick the addicted person out in a crowd.

Another common misconception is that someone who struggles with addiction became addicted because of a traumatic event. This person's mind has been broken. This is not necessarily true. Some have lived totally "normal" lives with loving parents and families. They have a good education and great career. Experiencing trauma does increase the chance of becoming addicted and being addicted increases the chance of experiencing trauma. It really doesn't matter how or why a person started experimenting with their poison. It doesn't matter how or why YOU got to the place you are. You're here now and that's what is important. You are not alone.

> *No temptation has overtaken you except what is common to mankind. And God is faithful; he will not let you be tempted beyond what you can bear. But when you are tempted, he will also provide a way out so that you can endure it. (1 Corinthians, 10:13 NIV)*

Many times, when facilitating group meetings and during one-on-one sessions, I've heard the phrase "God is testing me" and "God tested me". If you share this belief, I want to point out that addictions are not at all God's way of testing you. They are one of the tricks Satan uses to pull you further away from your Father. Think about it for a minute. Do you regularly attend church? Spend quality time with other people of faith? Do you lie to cover your behaviors? Defile the body God gave you by putting harmful substances inside of it? Commit adultery? Theft? Many sinful behaviors commonly occur when a person is struggling with an addiction. This sounds harsh, but while you are living an addicted lifestyle, you are bowing to the father of lies instead of to the Father of Truth and Love. You are submitting yourself to the desires of the world instead of your Father above.

> *You belong to your father, the devil, and you want to carry out your father's desires. He was a murderer from the beginning, not holding to the truth, for there is no truth in him. When he lies, he speaks his native language, for he is a liar and the father of lies. (John 8:44, NIV)*

> *13 When tempted, no one should say, "God is tempting me." For God cannot be tempted*
> *by evil, nor does he tempt anyone; 14 but each person is tempted when they are dragged*
> *away by their own evil desire and enticed. 15 Then, after desire has conceived, it gives*
> *birth to sin; and sin, when it is full-grown, gives birth to death. 16 Don't be deceived,*
> *my dear brothers and sisters. 17 Every good and perfect gift is from above, coming down*
> *from the Father of the heavenly lights, who does not change like shifting shadows. 18 He*
> *chose to give us birth through the word of truth, that we might be a kind of firstfruits of*
> *all he created. (James 1:13-18, NIV)*

God did not give you instructions in caring for your body and follow them up by using it to test you. He created an intricate masterpiece when He knit you together in your mothers womb. An example of what scripture says about your body is this:

> *19 Do you not know that your bodies are temples of the Holy Spirit, who is in you,*
> *whom you have received from God? You are not your own; 20 you were bought at a price.*
> *Therefore honor God with your bodies. (1 Corinthians 6:19-20, NIV)*

He did not give you instructions in using your own mind and follow them up by using it to test you either. He gave you a mind capable of thinking things through and making your own decisions. A few examples of what scripture says about your mind are these:

> *13 Therefore, with minds that are alert and fully sober, set your hope on the grace to be*
> *brought to you when Jesus Christ is revealed at his coming. 14 As obedient children, do*
> *not conform to the evil desires you had when you lived in ignorance. (1 Peter 1:13-14,*
> *NIV)*

> *8 Be alert and of sober mind. Your enemy the devil prowls around like a roaring lion*
> *looking for someone to devour. 9 Resist him, standing firm in the faith, because you*
> *know that the family of believers throughout the world is undergoing the same kind of*
> *sufferings. (1 Peter 5:8-9, NIV)*

The Cost of Addiction

When living in your addicted world, Satan fills your brain with lie after lie. He makes you believe that your vice isn't hurting anyone, even yourself. For a while, you believe this. You may not see the extent of what your addiction has cost you. Flushing money down the toilet to obtain your vice is obvious, but have you ever calculated how much money you have actually spent? How much money have you wasted trying to cover up your habit? How much have you lost due to missed work and not getting raises or promotions because of your addiction. This one may be hard to answer. You might not even be aware that your addiction caused you to lose these things, but having hangovers, withdrawal, being late for work, inappropriate attitude, poor work ethic, inability to concentrate because you're thinking of your vice, etc. can all affect your job performance, which in turn affects raises and promotions.

These issues can also affect relationships with those around you. Thinking back, have you lost or nearly lost any close relationships during your life of addiction? Your thought process and ability to recognize inappropriate behaviors and attitudes during addiction differ from healthy, sober thought processes. While in the addicted phase, you don't always see that what you did or said was wrong. To your mind, the main goal is getting temporary satisfaction and those are the thoughts that drive you. At this point, you're driving on flat tires and you're not going to get very far until you change them or fix the leak.

At some point you may have experienced embarrassment and guilt because of your addiction.

At some point you may have experienced embarrassment and guilt because of your addiction. Perhaps another price you have paid is the loss of dignity due to actions that were less than appealing. You may have paid the price of loss of respect from those around you.

After experiencing all these losses, you have probably even paid with the loss of self-esteem. Mentally and emotionally, you may have suffered from depression, anxiety and other social issues, which are just a few additional prices you have paid to your addiction.

Addictions have the ability to cheat you out of good health too. Introducing chemicals into your body can produce a multitude of problematic medical conditions, some life threatening. Nonchemical related addictions such as gambling, social media, love, sex, etc., can have medical consequences as well. High blood pressure (which may lead to stroke), intestinal issues and migraines are just a few of the physical repercussions people experience.

As you can see, continuing to live your life in the addicted phase is like driving on flat tires. You aren't getting anywhere that you want to go, you aren't getting anything in life that you truly desire, and you aren't becoming the person you want to be. Now that you are ready to air your tires up or change them entirely, you'll begin to see major changes in every aspect of your life.

From this point forward, we're going to refer to your vice as "Bill". Seems fitting, right? After all, you've paid dearly to it.

Let's take a little bit of time to think of any and every price you have paid to your addiction. If you struggle with multiple addictions, you may need to focus on the one causing your life the most damage first, then go back and tackle the others. Complete the receipt at the end of this chapter and you will have a better idea of how expensive it has been. Get detailed. Name each person, job, opportunity, emotion, negative aspect, etc. that Bill has cost you. Use additional paper if needed and include other miscellaneous items. Much like every person I have coached, when I first listed out the expenses, I missed things. Even today, I have "aha" moments that serve as great reminders of the price I myself have paid.

After reviewing all of the paid items on your receipt, spend a little bit of time considering what you will be able to accomplish once you have fully aired tires and you're on your way to your destination of happiness.

Paid to Bill Worksheet

The Price of My Addiction

From Beginning _____________ To Current _____________

Money spent (Include cost of Bill, list cost to get Bill such as gas/internet/etc.):

____

____

____

____

Relationships:

____

____

____

____

____

____

____

Jobs/Job Opportunities (Include opportunities lost because of inability to pass drug test):

____

____

____

____

____

Material Items (Include items lost or unable to obtain due to financial payments to Bill):

Social Opportunities:

Emotional and Mental Expenses:

Health Related:

Chapter 3

Parking in the Middle of the Road Indecision & Inaction

Not making a decision or taking action is like parking in the middle of the road. You're going nowhere, just sitting there waiting to get rear ended, broadsided or hit head on by someone else.

I was always a horrible decision maker. Not because I always made bad decisions (although I made a lot of bad decisions), but because I put off making a decision to begin with. I avoided making decisions because I wasn't sure how it would turn out. Especially when faced with more than one option. I would think and consider, then think and consider more, but found it almost impossible to make a definitive decision and take action.

The truth is, not making a decision is, in fact, making a decision. It is deciding to not act, therefore, letting other people or your environment make the decision for you. Let's imagine you didn't decide whether or not to take that class you needed for a promotion to advance your career. Now your employer has decided that you're going to stay in the mediocre position that you absolutely hate. By not deciding for yourself, you made the decision to let someone else make the decision about your career. How do you feel about someone or something telling you what to do? Wouldn't you rather do whatever it is you want to do instead of what someone else says you're going to do? Letting someone else make your decision may seem like it's easier, but it's only easier in that moment. The decision they make for you will most likely not lead you to your Destination Happiness.

Now let's imagine that although you've thought about it, you haven't made the decision to stop participating in your addiction. Perhaps you've given it a great deal of consideration but haven't quite committed to the decision to do so. By not making the decision to stop, you have in fact, decided to not stop.

Indecision is actually a form of self-abuse.

Indecision is actually a form of self-abuse. Being indecisive is the ultimate form of giving away your power. Your decisions are what determine your future and if someone or something else is making them for you, they are determining your future. Do you trust them to make the right decisions for you? To me, the saddest thing about indecision is when you know what you wanted yet let it slip away.

Since you're reading this book, I'm going to assume you want to make changes in your life that will require you to make a lot of decisions along the way. In your quest for an addiction free, happy life you're going to find yourself faced with choices that will either launch you forward or hold you back. The number one most important decision for you at this moment is this: are you going to quit? Not do you want to. Not should you. Not are you ready to. Are you going to?

> *19 "Today I have given you the choice between life and death, between blessings and curses. Now I call on heaven and earth to witness the choice you make. Oh, that you would choose life, so that you and your descendants might live! 20 You can make this choice by loving the Lord your God, obeying him, and committing yourself firmly to him. This is the key to your life. And if you love and obey the Lord, you will live long in the land the Lord swore to give your ancestors Abraham, Isaac, and Jacob." (Deuteronomy 30:19-20, NLT)*

What you do in life speaks so loudly that others can barely hear what you say.

Being a Christian means more than simply believing and having faith. It means living a Christ centered life. As a Christian, every decision you make should be based on Christian values. What you do in life speaks so loudly that others can barely hear what you say. Your life should speak in such a way that people around you can clearly see that you walk with God.

> *7 Above all, set yourself apart as a model of a life nobly lived. With dignity, demonstrate integrity in all that you teach. 8 Bring a clear, wholesome message that cannot be condemned, and then your critics will be embarrassed, with nothing bad to say about us. (Titus 2:7-8, TPT)*

Keep in mind that your decisions are yours alone. Yours to control. Nobody else can make them for you unless you allow them to. Now it's time to make this decision. The curve to the left will continue to take you further from God and will be covered in puddles and mud holes of sin. You'll continue your negative behaviors. The same ones you know you want to give up. You won't find happiness on this road because you will be overwhelmed by feelings of guilt and shame. You know in your heart that this isn't the road that's best for you and it isn't the road God wants you to follow.

The road to the right leads to more happiness than you have ever experienced in the life of your addiction. You will find real relationships, true confidence, increased self-image, spiritual awareness and you will be able to enjoy a positive outlook on life. So, which road do you choose? Are you going to quit?

Inaction

You've made the decision to keep reading. Fantastic! You're steering in the right direction.

During the days of drinking myself into oblivion, I knew I needed to quit. I wanted to quit. I eventually made the decision to quit. At the same time, I made excuse after excuse that kept me from taking action. We'll discuss the excuses we use later in the chapter titled "Take Back the Wheel". The decision was made, but I couldn't seem to get myself to move.

Inaction held me in place again when after many months of arguing with God about my abilities and writing this book, I finally decided to agree to his command. I would write this book to help others through their addictions. Yet I still found myself parked in the middle of the road. I had decided that I would comply, but I wasn't taking action. I just sat there, be-bopping to the music while watching the cars go by. I noticed people inside the cars struggling to find their way, slowing down to look at the street signs with confused looks on their faces. Yet for a while, I still sat there. I knew what I needed to do but wasn't able to get myself to do it.

I needed a spark to get me moving and a fire to keep me going. Then I decided to start applying the 5 second rule. Anytime I make a decision to do something that is of value I strongly encourage myself to start within 5 seconds. I begin by counting backwards 5-4-3-2-MOVE. I don't think about it, I just move. The thought processes behind this are simple. Your brain is focused on the numbers as you're counting instead of what you are dreading and by counting backwards, you're signaling to your brain that there is an end to the time of inaction. This also works amazingly well when I'm dreading washing dishes or putting laundry away (hint, hint).

After teaching this in a group meeting, I had a member report to me that she implements the 5 second rule to get her out of less than desirable situations. One example was when she found herself surrounded by people that were trying to persuade her to get high with them. In that moment, her mind was whirling but she immediately remembered the 5 second rule. 5-4-3-2-GET AWAY.

Take a look at the following verses. In 1 Peter 3:11 we are given instructions to make a decision as well as to take action. Then look at what James teaches in chapter 4. I believe these verses are quite fitting when discussing the decision to give up your addiction and acting on that decision.

> *They must turn from evil and do good; they must seek peace and pursue it.*
> *(1 Peter 3:11, NIV)*

> *Remember, it is sin to know what you ought to do and then not do it.*
> *(James 4:17, NLT)*

Today, I ask you to make yourself three promises. 1) Promise that you will make decisions based on your Christian values. 2) Promise that you will take action immediately after the decision is made. 3) Promise to keep your momentum moving forward to bring these decisions to fruition.

For the next exercise, I would like for you to think about times when you let someone else or a circumstance make a decision for you. Include times that your inaction made the decision for you. Ask yourself these questions for each occurrence and write them down on the Reflections page.

1. What kept you from making the decision?
2. What might have been the outcome if you had made the decision for yourself and acted on it?
3. How might your life be different today?

haven't quite committed to the decision to do so. By not making the decision to stop, you have in fact, decided to not stop.

Indecision is actually a form of self-abuse.

Indecision is actually a form of self-abuse. Being indecisive is the ultimate form of giving away your power. Your decisions are what determine your future and if someone or something else is making them for you, they are determining your future. Do you trust them to make the right decisions for you? To me, the saddest thing about indecision is when you know what you wanted yet let it slip away.

Since you're reading this book, I'm going to assume you want to make changes in your life that will require you to make a lot of decisions along the way. In your quest for an addiction free, happy life you're going to find yourself faced with choices that will either launch you forward or hold you back. The number one most important decision for you at this moment is this: are you going to quit? Not do you want to. Not should you. Not are you ready to. Are you going to?

> *19 "Today I have given you the choice between life and death, between blessings and curses. Now I call on heaven and earth to witness the choice you make. Oh, that you would choose life, so that you and your descendants might live! 20 You can make this choice by loving the Lord your God, obeying him, and committing yourself firmly to him. This is the key to your life. And if you love and obey the Lord, you will live long in the land the Lord swore to give your ancestors Abraham, Isaac, and Jacob." (Deuteronomy 30:19-20, NLT)*

What you do in life speaks so loudly that others can barely hear what you say.

Being a Christian means more than simply believing and having faith. It means living a Christ centered life. As a Christian, every decision you make should be based on Christian values. What you do in life speaks so loudly that others can barely hear what you say. Your life should speak in such a way that people around you can clearly see that you walk with God.

> *7 Above all, set yourself apart as a model of a life nobly lived. With dignity, demonstrate integrity in all that you teach. 8 Bring a clear, wholesome message that cannot be condemned, and then your critics will be embarrassed, with nothing bad to say about us. (Titus 2:7-8, TPT)*

Chapter 3

Parking in the Middle of the Road Indecision & Inaction

Not making a decision or taking action is like parking in the middle of the road. You're going nowhere, just sitting there waiting to get rear ended, broadsided or hit head on by someone else.

I was always a horrible decision maker. Not because I always made bad decisions (although I made a lot of bad decisions), but because I put off making a decision to begin with. I avoided making decisions because I wasn't sure how it would turn out. Especially when faced with more than one option. I would think and consider, then think and consider more, but found it almost impossible to make a definitive decision and take action.

The truth is, not making a decision is, in fact, making a decision. It is deciding to not act, therefore, letting other people or your environment make the decision for you. Let's imagine you didn't decide whether or not to take that class you needed for a promotion to advance your career. Now your employer has decided that you're going to stay in the mediocre position that you absolutely hate. By not deciding for yourself, you made the decision to let someone else make the decision about your career. How do you feel about someone or something telling you what to do? Wouldn't you rather do whatever it is you want to do instead of what someone else says you're going to do? Letting someone else make your decision may seem like it's easier, but it's only easier in that moment. The decision they make for you will most likely not lead you to your Destination Happiness.

Now let's imagine that although you've thought about it, you haven't made the decision to stop participating in your addiction. Perhaps you've given it a great deal of consideration but

Chapter 4

Shift From Willpower to Faith Power

I knew I simply didn't have enough willpower to drive by the liquor or grocery store and not pick up a bottle. I thought that if I increased my willpower, I could skip that first drink in the evening. The one that led to another one. Then another one. Then more until I lied to myself again by saying, "this will be my last one."

We hear about willpower every day. "You just don't have enough willpower." or "I didn't have the willpower to resist." From a very young age, you were told that you could do anything you set your mind to. Oftentimes though, you realized that willpower wasn't enough and you gave up. You have already proven to yourself that your willpower isn't strong enough to overcome your desire to temporarily please yourself.

When most people think of willpower, they think restraint. Self-control. It's even referred to as a muscle that you can build. When I think of willpower I think pain, agony, deprivation, and restriction. These thoughts literally cause me to feel a void and make my chest heavy. I feel grief. Subsequently, this makes my desire for what I'm trying to avoid even stronger. It consumes my mind.

Before I stopped drinking, I would spend countless hours every day, often at night with a mixed spiced rum and cola within my reach, performing research online. I searched for every way imaginable to stop drinking. I checked out herbal supplements, group meetings, essential oils, online therapy, yoga, ways to increase my willpower, you name it. I was looking for an easy button. Instead, what I found was countless resources telling me how difficult it was going to be if my willpower wasn't strong enough. They led me to believe that I was going to be miserable for the rest of my life, fighting a constant battle of will. According to every resource I found, I would forever be an alcoholic (or recovering alcoholic). They gave me yet another excuse to drink. Hey, if I'm going to be miserable while trying to give up Bill and for the remainder of my days, why bother with trying to quit? I may as well be miserable while drinking and not have to go through the loss of my crutch, right? Wrong!

Willpower will not heal the heart. Your heart however, can heal your mind.

Our entire lives, we're taught that having willpower is having power. Mercy, what a lie! Your willpower is you trying to work it out in your mind. It's a battle of your thoughts. As humans, we tend to argue with ourselves instead of working it out in our hearts. Will = Mind. Heart = Spirit. Willpower will not heal the heart. Your heart however, can heal your mind.

Thanks to the serpent, Eve and Adam, we were born with sinful nature. There has only been one man to walk the Earth since its creation, that was free of sin. The one and only perfect, sinless person was Jesus and I can assure you, He didn't use willpower to remain righteous. Stay with me. Here's where it gets interesting. God gave you something much more powerful than willpower. He gave you Spirit Power. Thank you, Father!

> *For the Spirit God gave us does not make us timid, but gives us power, love and self-discipline. (2 Timothy 1:7, NIV)*

> *So he said to me, "This is the word of the Lord to Zerubbabel: 'Not by might nor by power, but by my Spirit,' says the Lord Almighty. (Zechariah 4:6, NIV)*

Shifting from willpower to Faith Power will enable the Holy Spirit to lead you where our Father wants you to go.

Your will is fueled by your flesh or "self". Your desires, impulses, etc., are also fueled by your flesh. Remember that your will = your mind. Your continued addiction is fueled by these desires, impulses, etc., leading your will wherever they want it to go. Essentially, trying to give up Bill using willpower is working against you. Shifting from willpower to Faith Power will enable the Holy Spirit to lead you where our Father wants you to go.

> *6 This is why we must not fall asleep, as the rest do, but keep wide awake and clearheaded. 7 For those who are asleep sleep the night away, and drunkards get drunk at night. 8 But since we belong to the day, we must stay alert and clearheaded by placing the breastplate of faith and love over our hearts, and a helmet of the hope of salvation over our thoughts. 9 For God has not destined us for wrath but to possess salvation through our Lord Jesus, the Anointed One. (1 Thessalonians 5:6-9, TPT)*

Willpower cannot change our hearts, but once you begin to allow the Spirit to take the lead, He can guide your will towards His thoughts, share His wisdom, and change your life. Complete metanoia (change in one's way of life resulting from penitence or spiritual conversion, change of heart).

> *16 So I say, walk by the Spirit, and you will not gratify the desires of the flesh. 17 For the flesh desires what is contrary to the Spirit, and the Spirit what is contrary to the flesh. They are in conflict with each other, so that you are not to do whatever you want. 18 But if you are led by the Spirit, you are not under the law. (Galatians 5:16-18, NIV)*

> *19 The behavior of the self-life is obvious: Sexual immorality, lustful thoughts, pornography, 20 chasing after things instead of God, manipulating others, hatred of those who get in your way, senseless arguments, resentment when others are favored, temper tantrums, angry quarrels, only thinking of yourself, being in love with your own opinions, 21 being envious of the blessings of others, murder, uncontrolled addictions, wild parties, and all other similar behavior. Haven't I already warned you that those who use their "freedom" for these things will not inherit the kingdom realm of God! 22–23 But the fruit produced by the Holy Spirit within you is divine love in all its varied expressions: joy that overflows, peace that subdues, patience that endures, kindness in action, a life full of virtue, faith that prevails, gentleness of heart, and strength of spirit. Never set the law above these qualities, for they are meant to be limitless. 24 Keep in mind that we who belong to Jesus Christ have already experienced crucifixion. For everything connected with our self-life was put to death on the cross and crucified with Messiah. 25 If the Spirit is the source of our life, we must also allow the Spirit to direct every aspect of our lives. (Galatians 5:19-25, TPT)*

Almost everything I read during my research indicated that I would always be an alcoholic. I would forever have an addiction to the bottle. In meetings, those who have been clean from their addiction for years will often still introduce themselves as an addict. They are told "once an addict, always an addict." Many of them still feel that they are addicted because they are attempting to abstain using willpower. Go back to the preface of this book and read again how I introduced myself. Notice that I did not claim to be an alcoholic or a recovering alcoholic. That's because I no longer am. God had given me everything I needed to overcome my addiction. I shifted from willpower to faith power, allowing my faith power to direct my will. I would love to say that I have the strength of a thousand oxen, but the truth is, I'm weak. Thanks to our Father, I have had absolutely no cravings for alcohol or desire to drink since the day I left Bill on the side of the road. He lent me His strength and He will do the same for you.

> *3 By his divine power, God has given us everything we need for living a godly life. We have received all of this by coming to know him, the one who called us to himself by means of his marvelous glory and excellence. 4 And because of his glory and excellence, he has given us great and precious promises. These are the promises that enable you to share his divine nature and escape the world's corruption caused by human desires. (2 Peter 1:3-4, NLT)*

It can be this easy for you too. Our Father has given you these tools as well. Keep reading. Keep acting on the decision to leave your Bill on the side of the road. You'll experience this for yourself by the time you get to the back cover.

Reflections

Chapter 5

Driving With God in the Lead

Doesn't it make you feel much safer to know God is in the pace car leading you in the right direction? He will always be with you throughout this journey. He will provide you with all of the strength you need. He is your Powerhouse! You absolutely must let Him stay ahead of you in the pace car!

> *23-26 Then he told them what they could expect for themselves: "Anyone who intends to come with me has to let me lead. You're not in the driver's seat—I am. Don't run from suffering; embrace it. Follow me and I'll show you how. Self-help is no help at all. Self-sacrifice is the way, my way, to finding yourself, your true self. What good would it do to get everything you want and lose you, the real you? If any of you is embarrassed with me and the way I'm leading you, know that the Son of Man will be far more embarrassed with you when he arrives in all his splendor in company with the Father and the holy angels. (Luke 9:23-26, MSG)*

> *28 Do you not know? Have you not heard? The Lord is the everlasting God, the Creator of the ends of the earth. He will not grow tired or weary, and his understanding no one can fathom. 29 He gives strength to the weary and increases the power of the weak. 30 Even youths grow tired and weary, and young men stumble and fall; 31 but those who hope in the Lord will renew their strength. They will soar on wings like eagles; they will run and not grow weary, they will walk and not be faint. (Isaiah 40:28-3,1 NIV)*

During my teenage years, I had turned my back on God. I thought He had abandoned me and I was angry, lost and afraid. The longer I was defiant, the more angry, lost and afraid I became. Once I realized that I could not fix my drinking problem and destructive behaviors alone, I started praying about it. I remember nights that I was so drunk that I could hardly balance myself, down on my knees, sobbing uncontrollably, pleading to God to either help me through my addiction or take my life.

This was a very confusing time for me because I prayed and begged for help, but it didn't seem like God was listening. I believed that He didn't find me worthy of saving. I despised myself and thought He must too. How could He love me when I was such a mess and so disobedient. I felt He had given up on me. Until the night I heard His gentle voice. "I have given you the tools because I love you child. You just need to use them."

You see, what we often do is pray about what we want or need, but we don't have faith that God will grant our request. I was praying, but I didn't BELIEVE that He was listening or willing to help. I was simply going through the motions. Much like Peter, when I thought about how strong the wind and waves were in my life, I became afraid and began to doubt ...and sink.

> *22 Immediately after this, Jesus insisted that his disciples get back into the boat and cross to the other side of the lake, while he sent the people home. 23 After sending them home, he went up into the hills by himself to pray. Night fell while he was there alone. 24 Meanwhile, the disciples were in trouble far away from land, for a strong wind had risen, and they were fighting heavy waves. 25 About three o'clock in the morning Jesus came toward them, walking on the water. 26 When the disciples saw him walking on the water, they were terrified. In their fear, they cried out, "It's a ghost!" 27 But Jesus spoke to them at once. "Don't be afraid," he said. "Take courage. I am Here!" 28 Then Peter called to him, "Lord, if it's really you, tell me to come to you, walking on the water." 29 "Yes, come," Jesus said. So Peter went over the side of the boat and walked on the water toward Jesus. 30 But when he saw the strong wind and the waves, he was terrified and began to sink. "Save me, Lord!" he shouted. 31 Jesus immediately reached out and grabbed him. "You have so little faith," Jesus said. "Why did you doubt me?" 32 When they climbed back into the boat, the wind stopped. (Matthew 14:22-32, NLT)*

All those years of facing away from Him had kept me from personally knowing Jesus. I wasn't going to church or reading the bible. I wasn't spending time with God at all except to beg. I had no faith. I knew the devil well though. I had been listening to his voice for years. His was the voice that told me I was unworthy and unloved. He had me convinced that I was a horrible person and would never be anything more than manure on the bottom of someone's shoe.

He's such a liar!

> *But I am afraid that just as Eve was deceived by the serpent's cunning, your minds may somehow be led astray from your sincere and pure devotion to Christ. (2 Corinthians 11:3, NIV)*

Yep! That's what happened in my situation. After hearing God's voice though, I began to have faith. I started to believe in myself as a child of God, deserving of acceptance and happiness. I knew then that He was with me and that my life was about to change forever.

> *5 "I am the sprouting vine and you're my branches. As you live in union with me as your source, fruitfulness will stream from within you—but when you live separated from me you are powerless. 6 If a person is separated from me, he is discarded; such branches are gathered up and thrown into the fire to be burned. 7 But if you live in life-union with me and if my words live powerfully within you—then you can ask whatever you desire and it will be done. (John 15:5-7, TPT)*

> *1 But now, O Jacob, listen to the Lord who created you. O Israel, the one who formed you says, "Do not be afraid, for I have ransomed you. I have called you by name; you are mine. 2 When you go through deep waters, I will be with you. When you go through rivers of difficulty, you will not drown. When you walk through the fire of oppression, you will not be burned up; the flames will not consume you. (Isaiah 43:1-2, NLT)*

Passages like these can be found throughout the bible. To have faith is more than simply believing in God, it's trusting Him. There is absolutely nothing that is bigger than our Father. There is no trouble that He cannot help you to overcome. There is no battle too fierce, no adversary too strong.

> *And without faith it is impossible to please God, because anyone who comes to him must believe that he exists and that he rewards those who earnestly seek him. (Hebrews 11:6, NIV)*

Accountability

Everybody needs someone or something to keep them accountable in staying on track. You can and should be your own accountability partner, but you will also need to collaborate

He wants you to take your troubles to Him and lean on Him for support.

with God. Especially during times when you feel weak, afraid or tempted. He wants you to take your troubles to Him and lean on Him for support. He knows not only what you have done and what you are currently doing, but your thoughts and feelings. He knows you better than you know yourself. There's no one more appropriate to go to for guidance. Remember, you are not alone.

> *Therefore, each one must answer for himself and give a personal account of his own life before God. (Romans 14:12, TPT)*

> *23 Search me, O God, and know my heart; test me and know my anxious thoughts. 24 Point out anything in me that offends you, and lead me along the path of everlasting life. (Psalm 139:23-24, NLT)*

Our Father loves you so much that He is a very forgiving Father. Scripture says that if you repent, you will be forgiven. As loving and forgiving as He is, He is also a God of Justice. Much like your parents when you were a child, He doesn't expect you to continue repeating the same behaviors after apologizing. You can't keep saying you're sorry and go out and do whatever you want just to come back and apologize again.

The words "God of Justice" sound a bit unpleasant, so please let me explain. God is Holy. He isn't capable of wrongdoing. He is also good, but a good judge that ignores crime isn't a good judge just like a good parent that ignores their child's wrongdoing isn't a good parent. Because God is Holy and good, He must be just. Reading through the Bible, we see instances where He has punished the evil and stood up for the oppressed. His laws were put into place out of love for us and this love helps to protect us with order in society. A good parent like our Father provides correction, direction and discipline. Through repentance, there may still be consequences for your actions, but by His mercy, you may not get the punishment you deserve.

To repent means to feel or express sincere regret or remorse about one's wrongdoing or sin. It's feeling it enough to change the behavior and prevent it from happening again. God doesn't want us to apologize out of obligation or fear of punishment. He asks for repentance from the heart out of love for Jesus and gratefulness for what He did for us on the cross. Scripture tells us that you will have to answer for your behaviors the day that Jesus returns.

> *For we must all appear before the judgment seat of Christ, so that each of us may receive what is due us for the things done while in the body, whether good or bad. (2 Corinthians 5:10, NIV)*

> *"Behold, I am coming quickly. I bring my reward with me to repay everyone according to their works. (Revelation 22:12, TPT)*

> *"He will wipe away every tear from their eyes and eliminate death entirely. No one will mourn or weep any longer. The pain of wounds will no longer exist, for the old order has ceased." (Revelation 21:4, TPT)*

How you live is a reflection of your faith and trust in God.

How you live is a reflection of your faith and trust in God. If you truly believe that you are loved and forgiven by Him, you desire to honor Him and this is the driving force behind everything you do. I'm sure that like me, you don't want to disappoint our Father. I'm looking forward to the day that I can sit at Jesus' feet, listening to stories the bible doesn't tell.

Ask yourself these things. Am I living in a way that would honor Jesus? Would He be pleased with my life as it is today? What would He say to me if He were to return today? If any of your answers are negative, it's time to make a change.

Just a note here, I'm so proud of you for getting this far in this book! You should be proud too! You've made the decision to continue on this journey and at this moment you are trusting that God will steer you in the right direction. He put this book in front of you. He is giving you the tools. You are using them. And He loves you! I can assure you He is having a proud Father moment!

Alright. Moving forward. On the next few pages, you're going to have the opportunity to assess your faith and where you place it. This is a very crucial step in your recovery. You owe it to yourself to give each question and answer consideration and be completely honest with yourself.

Faith Questionnaire Worksheet

Take a look at where you place your faith in times of trouble. Answer the following questions honestly.

1. When I find myself unhappy at work, how do I react?
    A. I say a quick prayer asking for guidance, understanding and patience.
    B. I complain to and with my coworkers.
    C. I complain to my spouse/significant other/family as soon as I get the chance.

2. How often do I pray?
    A. I pray each day during an allotted time and throughout the day when I feel the need.
    B. I pray sometimes, when I think about it or when I'm in trouble.
    C. I don't pray very often.

3. How much time do I spend reading the bible, spiritual growth lessons, etc?
    A. I spend a minimum of 15 minutes every day learning God's word.
    B. I read the bible and spiritual growth lessons once or twice a week.
    C. I'm not into reading.

4. How often do I attend church services?
    A. I go to church every week.
    B. I go to church a couple times a month.
    C. I go when I don't have something else to do.

5. When I struggle in life, what is the first thing I do?
    A. I turn to God in prayer and trust His word.
    B. I worry about things for a while, then pray about it.
    C. I worry about things and try to figure out a way to fix them on my own.

6. Who do I go to when I need help?
    A. I talk things through with other members of faith.
    B. I seek help from my circle of friends who are most like me.
    C. I rarely ask for help.

7. Where does God fall on my list of priorities?
    A. God is number 1. He is the most important part of my life.
    B. God is important, but my family comes first.
    C. I know He is there, but don't think about Him much.

8. What ways do I find to strengthen my faith?
    A. I pray, attend church and bible study, and listen to worship music all the time.
    B. I go to church and pray when I have time.
    C. I don't know how to strengthen my faith.

9. When I am faced with a difficult task, how do I react?
    A. I pray about it and have faith that God will help me with it.
    B. I jump in and make a mess of it.
    C. I don't even try. I'm just going to mess it up anyway.

10. How often do I talk about my faith and God to my friends?
    A. All the time. They know I am a believer.
    B. I make a comment once in a while.
    C. My friends would judge me if they knew I love God.

11. When I pray, what do I pray about?
    A. I ask for guidance, say prayers for others and thank God for his mercy and grace.
    B. It seems like I'm always asking for help.
    C. I don't know how to pray, so I don't very often.

12. When I think about quitting my poison:
    A. I have faith that God will help me through.
    B. I can rely on a program alone to help me.
    C. I'm too scared to think about it.

Now that you have given a little thought to the strength of your faith, you may see that there are areas where you are a little less trusting in God or your trust is misplaced. Questions where you answered anything other than "A" are areas where you may consider making changes.

During a recent teaching, my pastor said, "Being a Christian and not going to church is about as survivable as being married but never going home." In a broader sense, I believe that not being able to honestly answer "A" to every question above will cause you to suffer unnecessary turmoil in your life. It's as survivable as the scenario my Pastor spoke about. If you think about it, practicing all of the "A" answers IS going home.

I can't begin to describe the way every aspect of my life has changed since I began strengthening my own faith. I no longer struggle with addiction, anxiety, depression, relationships, career, or anything else that used to keep me from moving toward the finish line. I am now a genuinely happy person with a bright and positive outlook. You are on the right track to begin living your best life too.

As you continue to grow in your faith you will discover that He has given you many gifts of your own.

The answer to the question "how do I make the needed changes?" is simple. Start incorporating the answer "A" into your life. Increasing your bible time, church attendance and bible study will help you to understand God's mercy, grace and love for you. Spending time with other people that share your spiritual beliefs will help to intensify your faith. Joining others at Christian encounters, retreats and conferences are amazing experiences and will not only jumpstart your faith but are fantastic for tune-ups. When you learn about all of the gifts and strengths He has bestowed onto others, your trust in Him will grow. Spending time in prayer will help you to communicate your needs and gratefulness more effectively. As you continue to grow in your faith you will discover He has given you many gifts of your own.

> *"Do not be anxious about anything, but in everything by prayer and supplication with thanksgiving let your requests be made known to God." (Philippians 4:6, ESV)*

> *You can pray for anything, and if you have faith, you will receive it. (Matthew 21:22, NLT)*

Prayer should be a significant part of your daily routine. I read an article once that says there are about 850 references to prayer in God's Word. If it's mentioned that many times, you know it's important. I wholeheartedly believe He is listening for your voice. He's patiently waiting for you to call out to Him, asking for help. His desire is for you to want His guidance, love, support and healing. It doesn't have to be a long, drawn out, wordy kind of prayer.

Here's an example of what it could sound like. Feel free to memorize this prayer so that you have it in your mind when the need arises.

Dear Heavenly Father,

I come to you today in appreciation for the grace and mercy you have gifted me. I humbly ask that you continue to lead me in the direction that I need to travel to be closer to you. I pray that you will strengthen my heart and mind and help me through moments of unbelief. Please help me to live with unwavering faith, knowing that your plan for my life is great. I ask these things in Jesus' name. Amen

> *14 The Lord says, "I will rescue those who love me. I will protect those who trust in my name. 15 When they call on me, I will Answer; I will be with them in trouble. I will rescue and honor them. 16 I will reward them with a long life and give them my salvation." (Psalm 91:14-16, NLT)*

You might be thinking that you can't possibly fit these things into your schedule. You'll learn how to work through this thought further into this book.

Chapter 6

Your Destination Happiness

The one thing we all search for in life is happiness. We want jobs that we enjoy, relationships in which we feel loved, comfortable houses with heat and air, security, etc. We want these things because we are unhappy without them.

Studies have found that happiness helps us out in a lot of different aspects. Happy people are more productive and better at communicating as well as problem solving. Critical thinking almost doubles, as does creativity. They are better able to express themselves and get their point across, take in information and make decisions on the spot. They also come up with new ideas on how to deal with situations in life. Putting these things together means a happy person is more successful in their jobs. They have more friends and longer lasting relationships. They connect with people on a deeper level, so these relationships are more intimate. People that are happy or smile a lot tend to get more promotions at work.

Studies have also shown that happy people heal better and faster, including people with illnesses such as cancer. You see, what happens when you're happy is that certain chemicals and endorphins are released in your body which are very impactful in the healing process.

Desire

What makes people unhappy is when we focus on the lack of having something we think we need to make us happy. We are constantly reaching for something and when we get it, we're happy for a while. In time, having it becomes "normal", so it doesn't give us the feeling of joy anymore. Then we reach for more or for something new.

We're constantly being bombarded with desires. Sometimes, because of our society, these desires aren't even our own. They come from what other people think or what they tell us we should want or who we should be. Things such as having a hot rod car or an oversized house. Society says we need things like these for status or to show the world we're successful.

When we look at this from an addicted person's point of view, often what we see is we may not want to use or drink or gamble tonight, but our influences (or people in our circle) do, Since they want to, they think you should too, so now you feel a bit of pressure and you reach for Bill. You might choose to use Bill in that moment because you desire to fit in. Your desire, in that instance, isn't to get high. Your desire is to feel a sense of belonging and to maintain a relationship. You are creating false desires because in that instant, you feel you should act a certain way or do something based on what you think someone else wants in effort to avoid feeling rejected.

Addictions have the ability to hijack the pleasure and reward parts of your brain causing you to want more and more.

Addiction tells you that you have to have your poison to be happy. LIAR! Addictions do have an effect on your happiness. But not in the way they tell you. Addictions have the ability to hijack the pleasure and reward parts of your brain causing you to want more and more. It makes you believe you have to have Bill to feel joy. It also takes over your emotional danger circuits, making you feel anxious when you're not using so that you use in order to physically and emotionally feel better, not just for pleasure. It's like being stuck in a roundabout, driving in the same circle over and over and over. It isn't until you find your way out of the roundabout that you start getting to where you want to be.

Addictions are manipulative. Bill tricks you into thinking you need it to be happy. It starts with once, then just a little bit more, and even more until it makes you think you desire it. What you're really looking for isn't your poison. It is a feeling that, if you think about it, you really aren't getting from your drug of choice either. You use Bill to try to fill a void in your life. That void is happiness. However, your addiction is actually stealing your happiness. Have you noticed that the more you give in to your addiction, the more unhappy you become?

Think about your desires for a moment. You don't really desire Bill. You have no desire to act in ways that are less than admirable. You don't desire the feeling of helplessness your addiction creates. So what do you truly desire? You desire real happiness. You desire love and acceptance. You desire to feel good physically and emotionally. You desire to be satisfied with your job. You desire to feel safe. You desire to be proud of yourself. Notice that the things your addiction causes are all opposite of what you truly desire. Take away the artificial desire for Bill, and you're left with real, more healthy desires.

> *He grants the desires of those who fear him; he hears their cries for help and rescues them. (Psalm 145:19, NLT)*

Tips for arriving at happiness without listening to the false promises of addiction

I can't begin to tell you how much happiness you will gain in your life once you have left Bill in the rear-view mirror. Things start to fit into place and life comes together. While you're getting there though, use the following tips to not only move you closer to your happiness destination, but step closer to God along the way.

> *A cheerful heart is good medicine, but a broken spirit saps a person's strength. (Proverbs 17:22, NLT)*

Steer clear of drama!

One huge challenge in trying to increase your feelings of happiness is drama. Did you know that for some people, drama is more addictive than cocaine? Drama causes your body to constantly release adrenaline, the fight or flight endorphin as well as cortisol, a fight or flight hormone. Adrenaline and cortisol are NOT happiness hormones. They keep us on edge and prevent us from feeling joy.

So, let's say you're driving up your happiness highway and another car pulls over in front of you a little bit too close and almost hits you. You know that rush you get? That feeling of fear and immediate anxiety. You experience this fight or flight reaction because when you perceive you're in danger or you become stressed, your body releases adrenaline and cortisol, letting you know you need to take action. Then after the danger is over, your body gets back to normal and you relax a bit. Consider "drama" the car that pulls in front of you.

So now, let's say you complain a lot about your job, your significant other, whatever it is that you are unhappy with. Your friends and family complain to you about their life all the time too. Did you ever notice a feeling of unease during that time? Maybe a tense feeling? Complaining is a form of drama and whether you are the complainer or listener, you feel tense and uneasy because you have a trickle of adrenaline coursing through your body and your cortisol spikes.

People tend to connect by having similar things to talk about. Maybe you and Joe connect over Nascar or the NFL. Perhaps you connect by complaining about how much money your wives spend on shoes or that you think your boss sucks. Start paying attention to how your conversations "feel." Talking about things you enjoy releases happy hormones that help the conversation make you feel good. On the flip side, complaining steals your joy and can actually exhaust you.

So how do you break this pattern? Stop complaining. Find the bright side of situations and focus on that. I don't mean to simply stop complaining to those around you. Stop complaining to yourself too. Your internal dialog. When you convince your body that it doesn't need to release adrenaline and cortisol, you seriously feel better. Not only emotionally, but physically. You'll even have more energy.

Essentially, having pleasant conversations with other people helps them to become more happy too.

When your conversations become more positive, it literally rubs off on those you're talking to. Essentially, having pleasant conversations with other people helps them to become more happy too. And if you're in the middle of a conversation and it starts to slide sideways, redirect it. Straighten the tires back out so that you can stay in the correct lane. Take your power back!

This is actually a lot more difficult to do than it sounds since drama is so addictive. It's a process. The more you practice creating happy thoughts and conversations the more natural it becomes. Then you'll find yourself reveling in happiness instead of being addicted to drama.

> *Those who control their tongue will have a long life; opening your mouth can ruin everything. (Proverbs 13:3, NLT)*

> *Even fools are thought wise when they keep silent; with their mouths shut, they seem intelligent. (Proverbs 17:28, NLT)*

Live a meaningful life!

Another amazing way to increase your happiness is to live a meaningful life.

Another amazing way to increase your happiness is to live a meaningful life. By contributing to the lives of others you're making an impact on yourself and those around you. You're in a state of gratitude. You recognize that your attitude positively affects someone else, in turn, giving yourself a sense of accomplishment and pride. This causes the release of the happy hormones more consistently. It can be something small like giving someone a sincere compliment on a job well done, or teaching a workshop that is designed to empower the people that attend, or even coaching a kids ball team. A few things that have made a significant impact on my life are serving my church in various ways, facilitating a Living Free program for church members along with our community and filling the roles of Life Coach and Mentor to others.

> *If you are generous with the hungry and start giving yourselves to the down-and-out, Your lives will begin to glow in the darkness, your shadowed lives will be bathed in sunlight. (Isaiah 58:10, MSG)*

Find your passion!

Engaging in hobbies can be a threefold path to happiness. I hear people say all the time that they aren't good at anything or have no talent. I don't believe this for a second! We were all given different gifts in life. What I found with myself in the past, is that I had no idea what I was capable of doing, so I assumed I would fail at anything I tried. This fear kept me from having interest in just about anything outside of my box. In case you're wondering, no, I do not succeed at everything I try. I have created more messes that I care to admit, and it was a danger for anyone around when I attempted any type of sport. Now I continuously attempt a variety of activities to learn what brings me joy. Participating in your passion makes you happy. You don't have to be perfect at your hobby, just enjoy it.

How can a hobby be threefold, you ask? If your passion is sports, you can play in charity events or coach a team. If your passion happens to be crafty things, you can make things to give to those in need, donate your handmade items to fundraisers, or even sell them with the proceeds going to charity. If you enjoy working on cars, you can donate your time to help someone in need or participate in charity car events. You can turn any passion into compassion. The feeling of accomplishment due to helping others has added to your happiness, simply by participating in your passion.

The third aspect is the fact that when you immerse yourself in something that brings true joy, you spend less time, effort, thought and money on Bill. Finding your passion is a win, win, win situation. You made yourself happy by participating in your passion. You have a feeling of accomplishment from helping others. You also added all the benefits associated with NOT being addicted to your pocket full of happy. Don't forget to be passionate about finding healthy things to elicit joy too.

Mingle with happy!

Surround yourself with happy people. We have these things called mirror neurons in our brain that mimic something else. If you spend time with people that act joyful, these mirror neurons try to mimic them so you feel more happy. The same effect occurs when you spend time with people that are depressed or angry. It is said that we are the most similar to the five people we are around most. Spend a lot of time with those that have great faith, and notice that your faith increases as well.

Spend time with our Father!

The single best activity I have found to increase my own happiness is spending time with God.

The single best activity I have found to increase my own happiness is spending time with God. Taking just a few minutes a day to talk to Him about all the things running through my brain calms me. Find a quiet place or get out of bed a few minutes before other household members and sit in conversation. Feel free to speak to Him as though He is your best friend. After all, He should be. There's no drama when you talk to Him and you're able to say anything you want to say. You can clear your mind by letting it all out without fear of arguments or repercussions. Don't you wish every conversation was like this? Study bibles are also fantastic. Most have an index where you can look up topics that you may be struggling with and easily find scripture for insight.

> *May the God of hope fill you with all joy and peace in believing, so that by the power of the Holy Spirit you may abound in hope. (Romans 15:13, ESV)*

Be thankful!

Sometimes, it can be very easy to lose sight of what we have. Especially when life feels heavy and nothing seems to be going the way we want. Addicted persons often find it difficult to cope with loss and tend to suffer more loss because of their addiction. It really is a struggle. Some people give the advice of looking for the pot of gold at the end of the rainbow or the light at the end of the tunnel. This coping strategy actually encourages despair since you're looking for things you do not yet have. Instead, focus on what you do have. Gratitude releases the happiness hormones and can literally change your mood and outlook in a second flat. Be thankful for each and every little thing, person, opportunity and event in your life. You don't even realize all of the wonderful things you take for granted until you take inventory of the positive items you have. Even the job you hate is something to be thankful for. Without it, you don't have money to pay your debts or buy things you need. Try saying "I get to go to work" instead of "I have to go to work" for a while and watch your attitude change. Then give a shout-out to God for making these things possible. Everything you own and all of the people in your life are gifts from above. Be thankful also for the strength you possess. I understand that you don't always feel strong, but you're still trying and you've made it this far. That, my friend, is strength.

> *Give thanks in all circumstances; for this is God's will for you in Christ Jesus. (1 Thessalonians 5:18, NIV)*

> *12 I know what it is to be in need, and I know what it is to have plenty. I have learned the secret of being content in any and every situation, whether well fed or hungry, whether living in plenty or in want. 13 I can do all this through him who gives me strength. (Philippians 4:12-13, NIV)*

> *Every gift God freely gives us is good and perfect, streaming down from the Father of lights, who shines from the heavens with no hidden shadow or darkness and is never subject to change. (James 1:17, TPT)*

There are other simple ways of reaching your destination of happiness, which you will learn throughout this book. Until then, let's get creative with ideas to help you get there quickly and stay in the right lane.

Finding Happiness Worksheet

Today, I choose to avoid drama by: ______________________________

____

____

I can live a more meaningful life by getting involved with: ______________

____

____

Things I would like to try in order to find my passion are: ______________

____

____

Positive, happy people I can spend time with include: ________________

____

____

I can spend more time with my Father by: __________________________

____

____

A few things I used to complain about but am actually grateful for are: __________

____

____

Other things I can do to be more happy are: _______________________

____

____

Chapter 7

Your Fuel - Motivation

Motivation can be defined as the reason behind your actions. For most, their addiction started because they experimented with something that induced a temporary feeling of pleasure. They would then try it again as an attempt to recreate that pleasure. Just a note here, achieving a sense of numbness can be considered pleasing to some people at times. Since the gratification isn't permanent and the "high" effects of Bill tend to lessen in effectiveness and longevity with regular use, they continually indulged to feel the pleasure until it became a routine. They are now falsely dependent on their Bill for a moment of satisfaction. The seeking of pleasure plus routine created a habit. The habit is now a physical and emotional addiction.

Habits are sometimes difficult to change. Depending on your Bill, you may also be afflicted by physical effects of your addiction that may make quitting even more challenging. **Withdrawal symptoms can be life threatening in some instances and I want to be very clear in saying that it is perfectly acceptable and extremely advisable to seek treatment from a doctor and/or treatment facility to help you overcome the physical challenges.**

Finding Your Fuel

People are always telling us what we should do. Our friends, family, co-workers, and kids all have their own idea of how you should be behaving. Even television commercials tell you what you should wear, what kind of car you should buy, who you should buy gas from, etc. If you pay attention, you'll notice that you're told what to do dozens of times every day. Fact is, you are not going to make changes in your life if you're doing it because someone

Motivation comes from your own desire, not someone else's.

else said you should. That isn't motivation enough. Motivation comes from your own desire, not someone else's. Let's say your husband gives you an ultimatum. "Stop drinking or I'm leaving you." That sounds like a good reason to stop drinking, right? But that is your husband's desire. Not your own. Yours would sound more like, "I'm going to overcome my drinking habit because I don't like my behaviors when I'm influenced by alcohol and I know my marriage and life will be so much better without it." It is possible to turn someone else's desire into your own and it is plausible for you to desire the same thing as the people in your life. The key is, it must truly be your desire and not what you think your desire should be because of someone else.

Any time you want to change something, you have to have a big enough reason to make the change. If you're not motivated enough or don't have the right motivation, chances are you won't follow through. If you've tried to loosen the grip of your addiction in the past and weren't able to, it may be because you didn't have a big enough reason or you were trying to make a change because of someone else's desire instead of your own.

Up to this point, you've been pretty passionate about Bill. Look at all the time, energy, effort and money you have invested in your addiction. One key to staying motivated is to be more passionate about living a clean life and reaching your Destination Happiness than you have been about Bill. A purpose that is greater than your addiction, so to speak, and something that is bigger than the obstacles you may face during recovery.

Spend some time thinking about what is fueling you to make life changes. Dig deep so that you get a true understanding of the REAL reasons you want to leave Bill in the dust. You may find it beneficial to read over the vision you created (chapter 1) and your receipt to Bill (chapter 2) before beginning. You'll find that there are several factors motivating you to make the changes. Although they may seem obvious, don't forget to include your spiritual reasons in the list. Spiritual motivations can help you in terms of defining your morals and values. Something to consider regarding the spiritual aspect of motivation is that you cannot serve both God and your addiction as John teaches us in 1 John.

> *15 Do not love this world nor the things it offers you, for when you love the world, you do not have the love of the Father in you. 16 For the world offers only a craving for physical pleasure, a craving for everything we see, and pride in our achievements and possessions. These are not from the Father, but are from this world. 17 And this world is fading away, along with everything that people crave. But anyone who does what pleases God will live forever. (1 John 2:15-17, NLT)*

It's time to find your fuel. You may want to get out a piece of paper or two. You will need to write your answers down. As always, be true to yourself by being honest.

Your Fuel - Motivation & Having a Big Enough Reason Worksheet

Consider the following and answer these questions honestly and as completely as possible. Make sure the answers pertain to your own desires and feelings, not someone else's.

The things about using ______________________ (insert addiction) that I am unhappy with are: ____

____

____

My life was better before I became addicted in the following ways: ______________

____

____

____

The worst things that could/will happen if I keep using ______________ (insert addiction) are: ____

____

____

Looking at the vision I created for my life, in what ways will continuing to use __________ (insert addiction) prevent me from turning my vision into reality? ______________

____

____

The outcome I will achieve by quitting ______________________ (insert addiction) is:

____

____

____

Emotionally, I will feel: ____

____

____

Physically, I will feel: ____

____

____

Quitting ____________ (insert addiction) will impact my life by (list all the ways it can/will impact your life): ____

____

____

If I don't quit ____________ (insert addiction), (list all the things that can/will happen if you don't quit): ____

____

Taking all of this into consideration, I desire to quit ____________ (insert addiction) because: ____

____

____

To me, this means: ____

____

____

This matters to me because: ____

____

Ask yourself "why" for each answer to the last question and each of those answers until you get to the core reason that you want to quit. This final answer is your racing fuel. It's the primary motivator to propel you to your goal. Keep this worksheet handy. You'll want to reflect on your answers periodically throughout this journey.

Note that your fuel may change from time to time. The more clean you start to live, the more clearly you begin to think, the more you realize what wondrous things you can accomplish. You may also currently have a motivator that is also an obtainable goal that you reach along the way so you'll want to find more fuel.

Chapter 8

Take Back the Wheel - Your Power

One of the most difficult things for me was accepting responsibility for my alcoholism. I endured a less than happy childhood which carried over into adulthood. It was easy for me to find fault in everything and almost everyone. It's so easy to say "I did this because of that". I could say that because of my childhood, I became addicted to acceptance which led to my addiction to alcohol, so it isn't my fault. That's an absurd thought though. In reality, I chose to drink. I chose to get stumbling drunk. I chose to ensure that I had enough alcohol on hand to make these things possible every single day. It was my choice. I could find excuse after excuse to drink. It's what we do when we have an addiction. What I didn't realize at the time was, my drinking habits actually created the excuses for me.

My thought patterns, emotional state and habits were all affected by my view of myself which made me want a drink and having that drink affected my own view of myself causing me to take another drink. I was spinning out, burning rubber and not going anywhere other than in circles.

Who do you blame for your current situation? A friend? Your significant other? Your boss? Parents? Do you blame yourself? So, here's what happens when you play the blame game. You spend so much time and energy focused on negative things that you don't have the time or energy to focus on what is good in your life or what you can do to make things better. You feel down, upset, heartbroken or even angry, which are all negative emotions instead of allowing yourself to feel happy, excited or empowered. You're not harming anyone else by blaming them. You're spinning your own wheels, holding yourself back.

You may also be giving your power to someone else by letting your thoughts about how they feel interfere with your progress. Let's think about this for a minute. Do you have certain people in your life holding a red flag in front of you? Are there people that aren't helping you get past the start line? Maybe they're creating too much drama. Perhaps they don't believe in you or they give you negative feedback.

Let me give you a little insight into these people. They don't want you to arrive at your destination! They may be afraid you're going to leave them behind. They may want to go with you but don't want to spend the time packing their luggage. Perhaps they don't want to go and they don't want you to go either because YOU are enabling THEM. Maybe they're in the parking lot with you and admitting that you have a problem would mean that they have to admit that they have a problem too. It could even be because you taking control of your life makes them question why they aren't improving their own but they're too afraid to try.

Making any decision based on what others think is, in fact, giving away your power. Do you ever find yourself behaving a certain way, doing things you don't really want to do or resisting change because of:

___ Fear of repercussions from others?
___ Guilt over hurting someone else?
___ Thinking someone else may disagree with your decision?
___ Feelings of guilt over disappointing someone?
___ Fear of being rejected, judged or criticized?
___ Fear of your life changing and leaving others behind?

How much of your power are you giving away to others? What is the correlation between the areas of your life that you are unhappy with and the areas of your life that you allow others' thoughts to determine? How different do you think your life would be if you took back your power and made your decisions based on what you know is right for you?

This is one time I'm going to tell you to ignore the red flag. Take back your power. Take the wheel and gently allow your tires to roll across the pavement. Don't look in the rearview mirror. Just drive. The folks holding the flag most likely don't realize themselves that they are toxic to you.

Outside Influence

Every treatment facility, counselor, pastor and support professional will tell you that you need to change your routines and people if you want to move past your addiction. God said it first in Proverbs.

> *Walk with the wise and become wise, for a companion of fools suffers harm. (Proverbs 13:20, NIV)*

> *Lovers of God give good advice to their friends, but the counsel of the wicked will lead them astray. (Proverbs 12:26, TPT)*

This may be the most difficult part of your healing process because you care about these people. Having love for them is the best reason to leave them behind. Think about it this way. You are working on overcoming something that causes hardship in your life, destructive behaviors, and emotional stagnation. Once you have made your journey and are on the path you want to take, you will be of greater value to them. You can help them overcome, model more positive behaviors, and have the emotional wellness to give greater love. Of course, this is dependent on your feelings towards them after you heal and their willingness and desire to be healed themselves. You may find that you care about them now because they fit into your life of addiction, where they may not fit later. I'm not telling you that it will be okay to climb back into a car with them. Always proceed with caution when around these people. You can be a positive role model in your own car driving a distance ahead of them. Always keep it in drive, gaining momentum. Never, never, never, shift into reverse or park. They'll keep up if they choose to.

> *4 Of course, your former friends are surprised when you no longer plunge into the flood
> of wild and destructive things they do. So they slander you. 5 But remember that they
> will have to face God, who stands ready to judge everyone, both the living and the dead.
> (1 Peter 4:4-5, NLT)*

Reasons for "But"

Now that we've discussed outside influences, let's talk about your own resistance to change, otherwise known as your "reason(s) for but." Sometimes, even though we want to change and we can see ourselves living a carefree happy life, we resist making changes. Why do we do this? Specifically, why are you doing this?

The most common reason is that change can be scary so you fear it. You get comfortable with the "known." This often prevents you from seeing another way of living your life. My motto is "Change is an opportunity for improvement."

Other common reasons are the fear of losing friends, losing your identity, and denying that your addiction is really an addiction. Trust me when I say once you have gained power over your addiction, you will have more healthy relationships, more positive behaviors, and you will look back at some of the crazy things you did while under the influence and realize your life was out of control.

Steering away from Satan's "buts"

> *"But" is Satan's word. He puts the word in your mind to keep you doubting.*

"But" is Satan's word. He puts the word in your mind to keep you doubting. It's how he gets you to do or not do whatever he wants to keep you trapped in behaviors that serve him. Have you ever noticed that "but" is usually followed up by a negative statement or an excuse? Think about it. "I cut someone off in traffic today almost causing an accident, but I was running late and had to get to work." "I shouldn't have spent most of the day on social media, but I was upset and didn't feel like working." "I shouldn't have spent my last $50 on drugs when my kids need school clothes, but I wouldn't have made it through the day without it." "I wish I had the courage and strength to stop drinking, but...."

Let's take a look at some common excuses Satan gives people to keep us trapped.

But it's too hard! Have you honestly tried? A lot of times, it's actually easier to do things you have fears about than it is to not do them. For example, say you want to stop doing Bill. Quitting your addiction is easier than using because once you quit, you don't have to use anymore. Continuing to indulge in Bill takes a lot more effort. Think of all the effort you have put into your addiction. Coming up with money to buy, finding a supplier, being nice to your supplier so that you can get Bill, going out of your way to get Bill, arguing with family, lying and covering up your habits and maybe even stealing. All of these things create stress and really take a lot of effort. So if you find yourself saying that it's too hard, remind yourself how much energy you're wasting on your addiction and focus that energy on more positive habits.

But it's going to take too long! How is it going to take too long? Isn't time going to pass anyway? It is your choice whether you're going to use your time repeating old behaviors or creating new, more desirable habits that are going to get you to where you want to be. As an example, for several years, I wanted to go back to school. I just thought it would take too long. Then it hit me. The program would take about 5 years. The same amount of time would pass with or without the degree. I might as well spend that time getting the education. Separating yourself from Bill will only take you longer if you continue to let it control you. The sooner you get into the driver's seat and take back the wheel, the sooner you'll reach your Destination Happiness.

But I don't have time! I'm going to call your bluff on this excuse! Think about it. How much time do you waste in a day? Facebook, games, TV? And let's not forget the time it takes to find, obtain and use Bill. So what other time could you use to think about building your super life highway? When you're in the shower? How about when you're driving home from work? Maybe get up fifteen minutes earlier in the morning to go over your plan for getting through the day, praying for help and reading affirmations you have created for yourself? Perhaps you take ten minutes before bedtime to reflect on the positive aspects of your day, give thanks to God and to notice how good it feels to have made it another ¼ mile up the highway towards your best life?

But my addiction is too strong! You're giving a lot of power to something that YOU control. Addiction does not have thoughts, feelings, behaviors or habits. It doesn't have anatomy to carry out basic physical or emotional functions. You are in the driver's seat, however you have given addiction the right to navigate by turning the wheel in whatever direction it wants you to go. Our Father has given you the authority to take that privilege away. Reach over and unlock the passenger door, open it up and kick addiction out!

But now isn't a good time. I'll try when the time is right. Awe, procrastination. So, when would be the perfect time? What do you need to stop your destructive habits? A job? Okay, do you now, or have you had a job while using? Did it cure your addiction? A relationship? Do

Truth is, being ready is merely an illusion.

you now, or have you had a relationship while using? Did the relationship cure your addiction? Less stress? Your addiction in fact, causes you more stress. More money? How much are you spending on your addiction? What could you be spending it on instead? Truth is, being ready is merely an illusion. Things in your life aren't going to put themselves in a perfectly straight line so that you can navigate easier. There are always going to be roadblocks that you'll have to get around. The best time is NOW. You will find that all of these obstacles will be easier to overcome once you're heading in a less dangerous direction.

But it's overwhelming! Let's look at what aspect of your journey is overwhelming. Is it time? We've already discussed this excuse. What sometimes happens is you look at your goals and getting from point A to point B can seem like a huge shift. It seems like it will require too much time, too much effort and way too much work. It scares the crap out of you! You're thinking, "This is so big and so overwhelming, and I'm never going to be able to do that. I don't know how I'm going to be able to handle it all!" Then what happens is, although you really, really want to be clean, sober, free and living a joyful life, it causes anxiety when you think about it. So what can you do to make it seem like less of an undertaking? Let's go back to your vision of that big, big picture at the end of the first chapter. Instead of thinking about all the little steps you're taking or need to take to drive up your highway, think about how you're going to feel when you get there. Once you can imagine how good it is going to feel when you have arrived, STOP thinking about it. Hit the brakes. Right there on that good feeling. Imagine it. Feel it. If you're having trouble feeling the joy and excitement, chunk your journey down into ¼ mile tracks. Focus your attention on each ¼ mile track, one at a time. Then revel in accomplishment after you've reached each ¼ mile. Lay on the horn! Slide, drift, do donuts in the middle of your road. Get excited that you made it another ¼ mile. Together with Jesus, you accomplished another task that keeps you traveling in the right direction. WOO HOO!

But I don't know where to start! Ummm... You've already taken the first steps. Look how far you've come. You've learned more about who God says you are, you've realized what your addiction is costing you, you've made the decision to continue reading and make changes in your life, you're learning to have faith and trust our Father in the pace car leading you forward, you've taken steps to increase your happiness, you've found your fuel and you're shutting Satan down. That is a lot of progress.

> *Don't you realize that you become the slave of whatever you choose to obey? You can be a slave to sin, which leads to death, or you can choose to obey God, which leads to righteous living. (Romans 6:16, NLT)*

Commitment

You've heard people say the phrases "Jesus take the wheel" and "Lay it down." I realized when randomly talking to people, that these phrases are often taken out of context. Some people believe them to mean that they should just let happen, what will happen. While this is true in some regard, God gave you the ability to make your own choices. He expects you to make decisions that lead to a more righteous life and closer walk with Him. He also commands you to be obedient to Him by doing what He tells you to do. Not dealing with an issue you are having and expecting it to magically resolve itself isn't how it works. He provides the instructions and the tools. You have to do the work.

During one of the courses I took, my instructor told a story that resonated with me. He saw a social media post of a friend about how frustrated she was about money. She said she wanted to become a millionaire. He started making some notes to help her reach her goal of becoming rich and sent her a list of ideas. Her response... "I'm not that committed. I just want to win the lottery." Do you think she'll ever become a millionaire if she doesn't want to commit to doing any work to reach her own goal?

What are the odds of you reaching your goals if you don't put in any effort into making it happen? It would be awesome if someone handed you a "get out of life's problems free" ticket, but I don't see that happening anytime soon. Besides, seeing the results of the work you have done is empowering. Thinking about the accomplishments I have made in my life gives me the warm fuzzy feels.

Do you fear commitment? A lot of people do because they misunderstand what commitment really is. Commitment is not "obligation." It's not something we should or have to do. Commitment is a choice. It is something we are determined to do because we have a genuine desire to make a change. Committing to doing something because you feel obligated is an inevitable head on collision. You're setting yourself up for failure if you're not genuinely dedicated to making the change because you WANT to.

When it comes to commitment in overcoming your addiction, you must be willing to quit and have the desire to quit. Addiction changes your behavior patterns and thought processes. Likewise, your thought processes and behavior patterns keep you tied to your addiction. You have to put your whole self into creating a new mindset that will lead to more positive behaviors. You can't pick and choose what suits you in this book based on your addicted mind frame and you can't pick and choose what you want to believe in scripture. God has never lied to you and neither will I. Simply reading this book and the Bible will not change your life. It only works if you take action. Give serious thought to the ideas and scripture presented and do the activities. Grab some highlighters to mark areas you especially want to remember. Get a few pens to take notes in the margins and complete the worksheets. The tools are only effective if you use them. If you skipped over the worksheets in the book before this chapter, this is a good time to go back and finish them. You'll get as much out of this book and the tools it contains as you put into them and there are no limits if you are committed to following through! I can't wait to hear about your progress!

While we're on the subject of worksheets, it's time to complete another one. The following worksheet will help you to understand the "buts" you have previously used to procrastinate or avoid leaving Bill on the side of the road. As always, be honest with yourself and dig deep. The second part is designed to help you see your addiction as it truly is. Something that you can and will regain power over.

Steering Away From Satan's "Buts" Worksheet

Which of the following "buts" are among your thoughts about stopping your addictive behavior? (Check all that apply)

___ But, it's too hard
___ But, I don't have time
___ But, I won't fit in
___ But, I'll lose friends
___ But, it's overwhelming
___ Other (List)
____

___ But, it will take too long
___ But, I don't have enough faithpower
___ But, other people may find out
___ But, my addiction is too strong
___ But, now isn't a good time to try
___ Other (List)
____

For each "but" you have used or are currently using, rewrite the "but" in the opposite and then write a positive affirmation statement. As an example, change "But, my addiction is too strong" to "My addiction is not strong. God has given me the power to win over my addiction" or "My addiction is weak. God is in control." Write as many positive affirmations as you can think of for each "but".

1. ______________________________
2. ______________________________
3. ______________________________
4. ______________________________
5. ______________________________
6. ______________________________
7. ______________________________
8. ______________________________
9. ______________________________
10. ______________________________

11. ______________________________

12. ______________________________

13. ______________________________

14. ______________________________

15. ______________________________

I hope this exercise has helped you to think of the power you have over your addiction differently. YOU and God have all the power you need to overcome any struggle you face in life. You can and you will win this battle!

> *Never doubt God's mighty power to work in you and accomplish all this. He will achieve infinitely more than your greatest request, your most unbelievable dream, and exceed your wildest imagination! He will outdo them all, for his miraculous power constantly energizes you. (Ephesians 3:20, TPT)*

Something you may find helpful is writing each of these positive affirmations out on a separate sheet of paper or sticky note and placing them in areas where you can easily access them when you feel a moment of weakness. Some people keep them in a pocket, in their car, on their nightstand, etc. I do not recommend placing them where they are in plain view all the time. My rationale for this is if you see them constantly, they may serve as a reminder of your addiction when you aren't even thinking of it. This keeps you focusing on Bill and all the trouble it gets you into instead of looking at what you're doing in that moment and the progress you are making. Just like drama, that quick glimpse in the rear-view mirror when you don't need to look back will cause a trickle of adrenaline. We'll write some other positive affirmations to keep in sight later in your journey.

Chapter 9

Release the Emergency Brake - Limiting Beliefs

God truly made us magnificent. All of our intricate pieces and parts fit together perfectly. Our brain is probably one of the most complex of His creations. Research shows that the average person has 12,000 to 70,000 thoughts in a day. Wow! That's a lot of thinking.

He designed us to deliberate, consider, envision, comprehend, conclude, contemplate, understand, imagine, and the list goes on. Our minds are constantly chatting away, one thought after another, some intertwined, some are positive thoughts and others not so much. One of my favorite verses regarding our mind is Philippians 4:8. Notice this verse contains the phrase "Fix your thoughts on what is true". Often, what we believe is true really isn't the truth at all. We, along with Satan, have convinced ourselves of the validity of these thoughts.

> *And now, dear brothers and sisters, one final thing. Fix your thoughts on what is true, and honorable, and right, and pure, and lovely, and admirable. Think about things that are excellent and worthy of praise. (Philippians 4:8, NLT)*

Have you ever sat in the driver's seat, put the car into gear, gave it some gas and the only thing that happened was the engine rev? Instead of moving forward, you stayed in place listening to the noise and wondered what was happening until you realized the emergency break was set? This can be frustrating and cause a moment of confusion. Especially when you're in a rush or are really excited to get to where you're going. Often, our mind is full of limiting beliefs that act like an emergency brake in our recovery, relationships, careers, really every aspect of our life.

If you're like a lot of people, there has been a time or two that you've wondered what makes you act like you do. Please allow me to explain. Our thoughts create our emotions and our emotions influence our behavior. They all interplay with each other. People say we should control our emotions and behaviors, but our power is in our thoughts since they are the foundation for our emotions and we behave based on how we feel.

Here's how it works. Your brain interprets everything around you. It then chooses a perspective or belief about the situation, which then creates an emotional reaction in your body. If the brain's perspective is negative, a negative emotional reaction will occur, and vice versa. Your body reacts to the emotion by releasing chemicals relating to that emotion. Sometimes though, our brain's perception is incorrect causing our emotional response to be different than it should be for that situation. As an example, you may feel sad while doing something that you normally get enjoyment from or anxious for no apparent reason.

What's happening is that your brain has learned a faulty pattern of thinking. It has been programmed by everything around you for your entire life and influenced by the thoughts and behaviors of everyone you're in contact with. Your parents, siblings, co-workers, friends, media, etc. have all affected the way your brain is wired. You usually don't even notice your thought patterns. Your belief system runs on autopilot.

Emotions are your body's reaction to what your brain is thinking. This is followed up with a behavior. Has there ever been a time when you misinterpreted a situation and behaved in a manner based on the misinterpretation only to find out later it was a misunderstanding? As an example, you went on a job interview and although by whom and when a call back would be made wasn't established, you expected a call in the next few days. The employer didn't call the next day and you thought that he/she wasn't interested in hiring you. This thought hurt your feelings and might have even made you angry. This emotion caused you to not call them to follow up and you took a lesser paying or less interesting job, ruining your chance to accept this position. Later you find out that they didn't call the next day because they were sick or had a family emergency or maybe even had to approve you as their prime candidate through the Human Resources Department.

Emotions are your body's reaction to what your brain is thinking.

An example of a positive thought would be your spouse bought you a puppy. Your brain perceived this as a wonderful gesture and triggered the emotion of love. The love emotion prompted you to hug, kiss, laugh, and all the other things love makes you want to do. On the flip side, if you wanted a cat instead of a puppy, your brain may have triggered the emotion of disappointment and your behaviors would have been totally different. Again, our behavior is based on our emotion and our emotion is triggered by our thoughts.

The behaviors you exhibit are a direct result of your thoughts. If you're doing things you don't like or aren't completely pleased with, your thoughts are to blame. The amazing thing about this is we can control our behaviors, by triggering more positive emotions just by changing our thought patterns. This can be challenging, but it can be done. It requires a little bit of mindfulness.

As I mentioned earlier, your thoughts are running on autopilot most of the time. You may not even realize you're having a thought or emotion. Until you know what you're thinking, feeling or doing, you'll have no way of changing it. As you become more self aware of what is going on in your subconscious, you'll regain your power. When you change the way you look at things, the things you're looking at change.

When you notice that you're having a negative emotion, stop and try to identify the thought behind it. What thought is making you feel this way? Once you have identified the thought, decide if it is 100% without a doubt true. Ask yourself "What else might be going on here?". Now that you're aware of it, you can choose a different interpretation. Once you have an alternate perspective, you'll notice your body feels different. Your brain is sending out a different chemical based on a new emotion. When you are happy or feeling a more positive emotion, you will change the decision you make regarding how you respond to the situation. You'll be more inclined to make healthier, more positive choices. Changing your decision and response will ultimately change the outcome, leading to life transformation.

> *Don't copy the behavior and customs of this world, but let God transform you into a new person by changing the way you think. Then you will learn to know God's will for you, which is good and pleasing and perfect. (Romans 12:2, NLT)*

Spend some time practicing this with both positive and negative emotions (see the worksheet at the end of this chapter). With enough practice, you'll be better able to recognize thoughts that lead to destructive behaviors and will be able to change your emotion before you act on it. This is extremely important when it comes to taking your power back from your addiction. Grab a few sticky notes and jot the following down. Leave them in places where you may need reminders.

Recognize Emotion → Identify Thought → Correct Thought → Change Emotion → Make Good Decision → Appropriate Action / Behavior → Positive Result / Outcome

As a side note, you may also want to know that your behaviors are guided by results of previous behaviors as well. They are learned responses. You may behave in the same way you have in the past because you think you'll get something out of it. When you were a child, you may have gotten rewarded for finishing a meal by getting dessert. You continued to finish meals throughout your life because you think you'll receive a reward. Perhaps at some point in life, you felt alone. You may have exhibited bad behavior or thrown a tantrum simply for attention and you continue to exhibit bad behaviors or throw tantrums because you think you'll receive this reward. Or you may have repeatedly engaged in less than desirable behaviors that earn you negative rewards because you feel you deserve to be punished. Rewards can look very different to people. Two that are common include sympathy and a victim identity. Again, these thoughts are on autopilot and are based on how the reward affects you emotionally.

> *5 Those who live according to the flesh have their minds set on what the flesh desires; but those who live in accordance with the Spirit have their minds set on what the Spirit desires. 6 The mind governed by the flesh is death, but the mind governed by the Spirit is life and peace. (Romans 8:5-6, NIV)*

Another tip to help turn a thought around is music. Have you ever noticed that an upbeat song makes you want to get out and scrub your tires with a toothbrush and a slower tempo helps you relax? The next time you're having a thought that is creating a negative emotion, try singing your favorite worship song. This will not only get the devil off your back for a while, it will change your whole outlook. You can also try putting a positive thought to music. Singing it helps you repeat the thought that you want to believe.

Since releasing our limiting beliefs is so important to every part of our lives and can be very difficult, we will continue this discussion in the next chapter. It's time to complete the worksheet.

Changing Emotions Worksheet

The emotion I am feeling is? ______________________________

The thought I am having that makes me feel this emotion is? ______________________________

____

____

What evidence is there that this thought is true? ______________________________

____

____

What evidence is there that this thought might not be true? ______________________________

____

Is the evidence based on facts or my feelings? ______________________________

____

Is the situation more complex than what I am assuming or are there other factors involved? What are they? ______________________________

____

Could I be misinterpreting the evidence or making unverified assumptions? ______________________________

____

Would other people interpret the situation differently? How? ______________________________

____

Am I looking at all of the evidence or just the evidence that supports what I already believe?

____

Am I exaggerating or thinking this way just because it's my habit? ____________________

Where did this thought come from? Who may have passed it on to me and are they a valuable source? ____________________

What may other people involved in this negative thought be thinking that is different from how I think they're thinking? ____________________

How can I look at the situation differently based on my answers above? ____________________

What is an appropriate emotion to the situation now? ____________________

How am I feeling physically because of this new emotion? ____________________

How am I feeling mentally because of this new emotion? ____________________

What is the appropriate action I should take based on the new emotion? ____________________

How is this action different from what I would have taken if I had not changed my thought?

____

How will this new action result in a better outcome? ____________________

Chapter 10

Accelerate Your Confidence

Confidence is a belief that you can accomplish something (or anything). It is being self-assured in your own abilities, knowing that even if you aren't good at something now, you can be if you put in a little effort and practice. It is a trust that you place in yourself and a trust that you place in God and the capabilities He has provided you with.

> *7 "But blessed is the one who trusts in the Lord, whose confidence is in him. 8 They will be like a tree planted by the water that sends out its roots by the stream. It does not fear when heat comes; its leaves are always green. It has no worries in a year of drought and never fails to bear fruit." (Jeremiah 17:7-8, NIV)*

Self doubt is the opposite of confidence. It is not having faith in yourself or God. It's like putting more faith in Satan's lies than God's promises. Self doubt is crippling, paralyzing you so that you cannot move forward. It keeps you from trying to win your battles and will keep you tied to your addiction. It blinds your mind to who God says you are, who He created you to be. Read over the first chapter of this book again if you need to refresh your memory about who God says you are.

> *13 For you created my inmost being; you knit me together in my mother's womb. 14 I praise you because I am fearfully and wonderfully made; your works are wonderful, I know that full well. (Psalm 139:13-14, NIV)*

> *Being confident of this, that he who began a good work in you will carry it on to completion until the day of Christ Jesus. (Philippians 1:6, NIV)*

Your Inner Critic

Numerous research articles show that about 80% of our thoughts are negative and up to 95% are repetitive. If you have 70,000 thoughts in a day and 80% of them are negative, you are averaging 56,000 negative thoughts in a day. If 95% of them are a repeat of a previous thought, you're repeating 53,200 negative things every day. That's a lot of negativity in your life. You could be repeating several negative things, or telling yourself the same few lies over and over again. Either way, this isn't a good scenario. Repeating a thought makes your brain believe it's true, even when presented with solid evidence that can prove it isn't.

Out of the 53,200 negative thoughts in your brain, how many of them do you think are Satan's "buts"? How many would you say are derogatory thoughts about yourself? We all have this little voice in our head that is a constant commentator. This inner voice can be our biggest cheerleader, motivating and encouraging us or our biggest critic, which puts us down and makes us feel inadequate.

Negative self-talk leaves you feeling discouraged, anxious and frustrated.

As an example, if you're always telling yourself that you're going to fail, you're probably going to fail. Negative self-talk leaves you feeling discouraged, anxious and frustrated. These negative feelings will impact how you act and the decisions you make. You may make poor choices, procrastinate making decisions or beginning a task, put in less effort or not even try at all. After all, your self-talk is telling you that you're going to fail so why bother to waste your time and effort trying? So in the end, you fail. But are you a failure? NO. Your inner critic is causing you to think you're a failure. This is just another way for Satan to keep you trapped and separate you from God.

Imagine for a minute that your little voice is screaming positive affirmations from the pit during the biggest race of your life. This encouragement makes you feel excited. You get pumped up and you begin to think of all the steps you're going to take to succeed. Your mind is telling you that you're going to do it and you're going to do such a fantastic job that you're going to win. Did you feel a difference in your emotions when reading this and the last paragraph?

Think about this for a moment. What percentage of time do you think your inner voice is speaking each of the following thoughts?

1. Criticizing yourself and/or speaking negatively to yourself?
2. Making excuses and/or blaming others?
3. Telling yourself that even if it doesn't work out as you want, things will turn out okay and encouraging yourself to learn from the situation?
4. Acknowledging that you can and will succeed?

A huge number of people have a very dominant inner critic. These thoughts are nothing more than a habit in thinking. Becoming aware of these thoughts can help you change your critic into a cheerleader.

So how do you recognize when your inner critic is taking over your thoughts? Here are a few ways to spot it.

Your critic is self-limiting. It loves to make excuses and say things like "I can't do this", "It's not possible," "It's too hard," "I don't have time", and other limiting statements. It shuts down possibilities before you even start due to fear of failure and humiliation.

Your critic makes assumptions. It believes it's always right, jumps to conclusions and thinks it can read other people's minds. It says things like, "He doesn't like me," "I'm going to make a fool of myself," and "People talk negatively about me." It makes up stories that aren't even true.

Your critic loves re-runs. It takes past memories and events and tries to turn them into a current day reality. It will replay negative experiences over and over in your mind and says things such as, "I'm such an idiot," "I never do anything right," and "This always happens." It keeps you at the starting line because it makes you believe you'll be unsuccessful because of the past.

Your critic may be someone else's thoughts. Remember that your inner dialog has been programmed by other people throughout your life. Since childhood, your parents, babysitters, teachers, coworkers, bosses, etc. have been inputting their words of criticism into your thought processes. If you think about it, you may be shocked at how many of your negative thoughts aren't even your own, but are based on something someone else once said to you.

Let's get a better look at your inner critic. Complete the following worksheet.

Spotting Your Inner Critic Worksheet

Self-Limiting:

What phrases does my inner critic say that sound like excuses to not stop using Bill? ______

____

____

What reasons does my inner critic give for these excuses? ______________________________

____

____

Assumptions:

What assumptions does my inner critic make regarding my ability to stop using Bill?______

____

____

What does my inner critic assume people will think about me? __________________________

____

____

What stories does my inner critic tell me that aren't true? ______________________________

____

____

Re-Runs:

What cynical thoughts have I been thinking repeatedly? _________________________________

____

____

What negative memories do I tend to think about over and over? ______________________

____

____

What judgmental phrases do I tend to say to myself or others frequently? ____________

____

____

Thoughts of Others':

When limiting thoughts come to mind, whose voice do I hear saying them? ____________

____

____

When analyzing each limiting belief of my inner critic, is the belief due to what someone else has said? (Yes or No) ____

____

____

Who said it (for each belief)? ____

____

____

Now that you can spot your critic, you can stop the negative thoughts in their tracks. You have a choice regarding your self-talk and you have the power to turn your critic into your cheerleader.

When you're in the middle of having a negative thought, it can be extremely difficult to think positively. Trust me, I know this all too well. Because our minds tend to repeat our thoughts, they have gained momentum like a truck rolling down a hill. You're so used to cynical thoughts rolling down that they've gained more and more momentum and now they're out of control. Your brain is accepting them as fact.

If you tell yourself that carrots are blue or elephants are green enough times, you may start to regard these statements as truth, although they're a lie. Likewise, if you repeatedly think that carrots are orange and elephants are gray, you'll accept these beliefs as the truths they are. The same principle applies in your beliefs about yourself.

Although you wouldn't want to step in front of the out of control belief truck to stop it, you can slow it down by putting a more positive thought in front of it. When you turn your thoughts about yourself into thoughts that are actually true, positive thoughts, you accelerate your confidence. Reminding yourself who God says you are and that He doesn't make mistakes will cause you to think the limiting thoughts less (if at all) and the negativity truck loses momentum. It will slow until it comes to a complete stop in its tracks. When I look back at some of the limiting thoughts I had about myself, I roll my eyes in disbelief that I could ever believe such lies. Silly me!

> *I pray that God, the source of hope, will fill you completely with joy and peace because you trust in him. Then you will overflow with confident hope through the power of the Holy Spirit. (Romans 15:13, NLT)*

For the next exercise, you're going to dispute the lies that fill your mind. It's time to uncover some truths about yourself. Now isn't the time to be humble. Be honest, but brag it up. Give yourself kudos and pat yourself on the back. Don't limit your responses to the lines on the worksheet. Use the margins or additional paper when you think of things that you don't have room to write.

Personal Asset Inventory Worksheet

What do I feel are my five (5) greatest strengths?

1. ____________________
2. ____________________
3. ____________________
4. ____________________
5. ____________________

What are three (3) things about myself and my accomplishments that I am proud of?

1. ____________________
2. ____________________
3. ____________________

What are three (3) challenges in my life that I have overcome and how did I overcome them?

1. ____________________
2. ____________________
3. ____________________

What are some unusual skills that I possess?

1. ____________________
2. ____________________
3. ____________________

What are some things people compliment me on?

1. ____________________

2. ____________________

3. ____________________

What are three (3) things I enjoy doing and/or am passionate about?

1. ____________________

2. ____________________

3. ____________________

What are three (3) ways I have made a difference in someone else's life?

1. ____________________

2. ____________________

3. ____________________

What five (5) things do I like most about myself?

1. ____________________

2. ____________________

3. ____________________

4. ____________________

5. ____________________

What are three (3) things my boss/coworkers would say they love about me?

1. ____________________

2. ____________________

3. ____________________

What are three (3) things my family/friends would say they love about me?

1. ______________________________

2. ______________________________

3. ______________________________

What areas of my life do I feel confident about and why am I confident in these areas?

1. ______________________________

2. ______________________________

3. ______________________________

What are five (5) things/tasks that I feel confident in completing?

1. ______________________________

2. ______________________________

3. ______________________________

4. ______________________________

5. ______________________________

Affirmations

Affirmations are statements that affirm or declare something is true. Earlier, we discussed how when you affirm something repeatedly in your mind, it becomes true to you, even when it is a lie in reality. One way for you to use positive affirmations is to redirect negative thoughts when they pop into your head. As soon as you hear your mind making a derogatory statement, state "That's a lie. The truth is..." and replace it with a more positive thought. Another useful tool is to use positive affirmations preemptively to beat the negative thoughts from surfacing to begin with. I suggest writing them down on brightly colored sticky notes and placing them in full view around the house, at your desk, in your car or wherever else you can think of. Read them every time you notice that colorful little piece of paper. It also works amazingly to record them on your phone and play various versions back to yourself at intervals throughout your day.

On the next few pages, you're going to write a list of positive affirmations. A note about your personal affirmations is that they shouldn't be farfetched. I mean, it really isn't going to be productive to write "I am Superman." when that's a fictional character. A more authentic statement might sound like "I am a superhero to my daughter." Looking at it from a child's point of view, their parents usually are superheroes (even though parents are all less than perfect), so this could be considered a true statement. You can also write the same concept multiple times in different words. Using the superhero statement, other versions could be "I am a superhero in my daughter's eyes," or "I am a father/mother that my daughter can rely on." You could even say, "I am the best parent to my daughter that I know how to be." Write it in your own words. See how many versions you can come up with.

A couple more notes about positive affirmations are as follows:

They should be personal. Use "I" "Me" statements.

They should be positive. Avoid using negative words like "don't," "can't," "not," etc.

They should be present tense. Avoid words like "will be." Write as if it's happening now.

They should be passionate. Put emotion in them. Get excited. Feel your words.

They should be written as a complete sentence. Avoid using abbreviations or skipping words.

They should be repeated regularly. Repetition of positive thoughts is instrumental in slowing the momentum of negativity and accelerating your confidence. A bonus in this process is that your belief system and thought processes become more optimistic, which will lead you closer to your destination of happiness.

Let's get started with your positive affirmations. Looking back at your Personal Asset Inventory Worksheet, write affirmations for each of your answers. As an example, let's say on the question that asked "What areas of my life do I feel confident about and why am I confident in these areas," you answered "I am confident at work." Your reasons were, "I am liked by my boss because I am always on time and get my work done." A few positive affirmations could be, "I am a dependable employee." "I am confident in completing my duties efficiently." "I am confident in getting my work done in a timely manner." "I am respected by my employer and coworkers." The list goes on depending on your positive attributes at work. Think about the "why" for each of your answers on that worksheet and write as many positive affirmations for each response as you can think of. Then envision every single other positive characteristic you possess and write affirmations for those. Also include affirmations related to your progress in recovery. Again, don't limit yourself to this worksheet. Use additional paper to make your list.

Once you have your list made, get out the sticky notes and recording app on your phone. Write and/or record each affirmation separately and scatter them everywhere! Have fun with this one!

> *4 Such is the confidence that we have through Christ toward God. 5 Not that we are sufficient in ourselves to claim anything as coming from us, but our sufficiency is from God. (2 Corinthians 3:4-5, ESV)*

Of course, absolute confidence comes from your confidence in Christ and who you are in Him. A worksheet for you to list your Christian Affirmations can be found at the end of this chapter. I have started filling it out for you, mostly based on what you've learned in previous chapters.

Beginning with a prayer is always a good idea. Ask God what He sees in you, and who He knows you to be. Ask Him to help you to see yourself as He does. Then take time to listen. Remember, if it isn't a loving response, it isn't God's voice.

Positive Affirmations Worksheet

1. I have control over the choices I make.
2. I am putting my life back together.
3. I have the power to make the best decisions for myself.
4. ______________________________
5. ______________________________
6. ______________________________
7. ______________________________
8. ______________________________
9. ______________________________
10. ______________________________
11. ______________________________
12. ______________________________
13. ______________________________
14. ______________________________
15. ______________________________
16. ______________________________
17. ______________________________
18. ______________________________
19. ______________________________
20. ______________________________

Christian Affirmations Worksheet

1. I am God's child
2. I am Jesus' friend
3. I am a member of Christ's family
4. I am complete
5. I am a citizen of Heaven
6. I am God's Masterpiece
7. I am forgiven
8. I am strong in Christ
9. I can do all through Jesus
10. I am accepted by Jesus
11. I am a branch of Jesus, the true vine
12. ______________________________
13. ______________________________
14. ______________________________
15. ______________________________
16. ______________________________
17. ______________________________
18. ______________________________
19. ______________________________
20. ______________________________

Chapter 11

Run Over Fear

Many nights you could find me on my knees. Uncontrollably sobbing out my prayers. Tears rolling off my face, snot running down my chin. Ugly crying. And let me assure you, when this face ugly cries, it is U-G-L-Y. Hours of searching the internet for an easy button to help me quit drinking led to story after story of agony. I was afraid. Scared of what would happen to me if I didn't stop, yet too frightened to try. During the day when I was sober, my mind was chaotic. It was full of concerns and questions. Who would I be if I stopped drinking? What would happen in my relationships since most of my friends drank almost daily too? The same friends that told me that I didn't have a problem. The very friends that would convince me to go out to have just one, then another. Would I fit in anywhere? Even my coworkers were drinkers. How would I cope with life's struggles? Would I be giving up more than just alcohol? Would I be giving up my life? I would work myself up into a tizzy and the first thing I would do when I got home every evening was to mix a drink to calm my mind and nerves. I wanted to stop drinking but I was petrified of change!

Fear has so much more power than we think. We unknowingly give it substantial control over our thoughts, emotions and lives. It causes us to assume the worst possible outcome in a situation, closing our minds to all of the positive things that God could make happen if we just allow it. It produces negative results and binds us even tighter to our addictions. Fear is caused by things that take us outside our comfort zone. Like change, for example. Anything that takes us outside our place of security makes us scream out "wait a minute? What's this? Is this a threat?". Even if you are desperate to make life changes, the thought of changing your behaviors and not living in addiction is viewed as a threat.

One very important fact that I want to point out is that fear is not an emotion given to us by our Father. It is another one of those lies from Satan. The bible specifically tells us this.

> *For God has not given us a spirit of fear and timidity, but of power, love, and self-discipline. (2 Timothy 1:7, NLT)*

God actually tells us not to be afraid in scripture such as Isaiah 41. Notice that He says He will give us strength and that we will be victorious. When we let our fear dictate our actions and hold us back, we aren't putting our faith in what He has promised us. We aren't trusting Him.

> *Don't be afraid, for I am with you. Don't be discouraged, for I am your God. I will strengthen you and help you. I will hold you up with my victorious right hand. (Isaiah 41:10, NLT)*

Have you ever really thought about the story of Jesus walking on water? I know we read this earlier in this book but it's worth reading again. Here is Matthew's account in The Passion Translation. Once you've read it, read versus 30 through 32 a second time.

> *22 As soon as the people were fed, Jesus told his disciples to get into their boat and to go to*
> *the other side of the lake while he stayed behind to dismiss the people. 23 After the crowds*
> *dispersed, Jesus went up into the hills to pray. And as night fell he was there praying*
> *alone. 24 But the disciples, who were now in the middle of the lake, ran into trouble, for*
> *their boat was tossed about by the high winds and heavy seas. 25 At about four o'clock in*
> *the morning, Jesus came to them, walking on the waves! 26 When the disciples saw him*
> *walking on top of the water, they were terrified and screamed, "A ghost!" 27 Then Jesus*
> *said, "Be brave and don't be afraid. I am here!" 28 Peter shouted out, "Lord, if it's really*
> *you, then have me join you on the water!" 29"Come and join me," Jesus replied. So Peter*
> *stepped out onto the water and began to walk toward Jesus. 30 But when he realized*
> *how high the waves were, he became frightened and started to sink. "Save me, Lord!"*
> *he cried out. 31 Jesus immediately stretched out his hand and lifted him up and said,*
> *"What little faith you have! Why would you let doubt win?" 32 And the very moment*
> *they both stepped into the boat, the raging wind ceased. (Matthew 14:22-32, TPT)*

Oh, how I love this story! The entire time I was under Bill's influence, I was Peter. I'm most likely correct in saying that you are too. I had no faith in my ability to quit. I had no faith that

God could or even would help me. I was so focused on the problem that I was unable to see the solution.

In Matthew's version of the story, Peter's problem wasn't the storm. It wasn't the wind or the water. It was Peter himself. He was safe while he had faith in Jesus, but as soon as the wind and waves distracted him his fear caused him to be focused on the problems instead of Jesus. His fear overrode his faith in that moment and could have resulted in him drowning. He asked Jesus to save him and Jesus took him by the hand and helped him back to safety.

Instead of looking at your addiction, focus on the solution.

You know what I'm about to say, right? Instead of looking at your addiction, focus on the solution. The more confident you are in Jesus, the more confident you will be with yourself. The more confidence you have, the less you'll feel fear. The less afraid you are the more confident you'll be. As your confidence grows, your chances of success in your journey increase. As you can see from this loop, confidence in Jesus is powerful stuff!

Fear of Other's Opinions

Another thing that tends to lay around in the middle of the road is our fear of other people's opinions. Caring about what someone else thinks can be positive in some aspects, such as when it encourages us to become a better human. But often, even when we should be encouraged, we see their opinion as an attack on our character or as if we aren't good enough. Sometimes, because of your internal critic, you make assumptions that someone perceives you a certain way, when in fact, that thought is yours alone.

When this happens, you are again putting more confidence in someone else's judgment of you than you are of your own opinion of yourself and your Father's. You're giving away your power and offending your Father.

Let me tell you a few truths about other people's opinions. The first thing for you to realize is that most people aren't analyzing you the way you think they are. Yes, you have a person or two in your life that are sitting in the bleachers waiting for you to make a wrong turn. These are most likely the people that have been tormented by Bill, right alongside you. They are hurt and angry. They still believe that you are driving on flat tires. These few people aren't the majority though. Most of the people you come in contact with aren't even thinking about Bill or your behaviors. They may not even realize that you have been struggling with an addiction at all. In their minds, you're a nice guy/gal. They notice the things you listed on your Personal Asset Inventory and Positive Affirmations worksheets.

When dealing with those around you that are negative or critical you have two options. 1. Lessen your exposure to them. This can be done with tact and care and doesn't necessarily have to be permanent. 2. If you're unable to lessen your exposure because they are too close to your life, you're going to have to talk to them. Listen to how they feel and why they feel the way they do. Offer sincere apologies for things you may have done to give them reason to feel as they do. And let them know that you are changing and that with time and their support you WILL make it through this. If they are unable to be supportive of your journey, you may have to go back to number 1. I know that sounds ridiculously harsh, but you aren't going to get to your Destination Happiness if you have people sabotaging your car or you can't see past them to notice God in front of you, leading the way.

I'm going to be honest with you here for a minute and tell you that someone else's opinion about you doesn't really matter anyway. Your life is between you and God. His opinion is the one that matters. Look at what Jesus does as explained by John pertaining to the woman who committed adultery.

> *7 They kept demanding an answer, so he stood up again and said, "All right, but let the one who has never sinned throw the first stone!" 8 Then he stooped down again and wrote in the dust. 9 When the accusers heard this, they slipped away one by one, beginning with the oldest, until only Jesus was left in the middle of the crowd with the woman. 10 Then Jesus stood up again and said to the woman, "Where are your accusers? Didn't even one of them condemn you?" 11 "No, Lord," she said. And Jesus said, "Neither do I. Go and sin no more." (John 8:7-11, NLT)*

While we're on this topic, it would be a good idea to find people and groups of people that are more positive and supportive. Your church is a great place to look. I know, you're thinking you would be embarrassed or ashamed for these people to know you on a more personal level than they do. You want to know the secret to developing relationships? Good because I was planning to tell you anyway. Stop putting others on a pedestal! There it is! Just like you and I, everyone has demons. Not everyone that appears to be happy truly is. Not everyone that seems to have their life together actually does. You don't see their life from the inside.

You may build a relationship with someone whose life isn't perfect but is a bit more put together than yours, but you didn't see all the work and effort that they have put into making and keeping it that way. Every human being on the planet has fought their way out of some sort of struggle. These people are your mentors. Having these people who are also Christians in your life will help you to maintain your walk with God and encourage you with biblical principles and ethics. Christians want to see people succeed.

I'm sharing a verse from Proverbs here, but you should read or reread chapter 12 in its entirety. There's a lot of good stuff about the kind of people we should surround ourselves with as well as strive to be.

> *Worry weighs a person down; an encouraging word cheers a person up. (Proverbs 12:25, NLT)*

Before we move on to the topic of change cycles, take a few minutes to reflect on the following questions.

What if Worksheet

What would happen if I choose to not use Bill? ______________________________

____

____

What would happen if I successfully stop using Bill? __________________________

____

____

What would happen if amazing opportunities start coming my way? ______________

____

____

What if I start to have better relationships with my spouse, kids, family and friends?

____

____

What if I can do the things I really want to do? ______________________________

____

____

What if this creates joy and happiness in my life that I never imagined possible? ________

____

____

What if I can live a life with purpose? ____________________________________

____

____

Chapter 12

Steer Out of the Change Cycle Roundabout

We want to say that our circumstances are to blame for our lives being what they are, when in reality it is our attitude and emotions that determine our behaviors and willingness to change. Fortunately, YOU determine your attitude.

Change is an opportunity for improvement, but it can be difficult to navigate. Often, we get stuck in the change cycle roundabout because we keep following the same path over and over again.

It is normal to resist change because often, we fear it. It has a lot to do with our perception of the change we are thinking about making. What you don't always see though, is that you are constantly changing. You adapt to different situations all the time without even thinking about it. It's automatic.

The first *Stages of Change model* was developed by James Prochaska and Carlo DiClemente in the 1980's. Now, you can now find several different change cycle models, ranging from four to seven stages. This is my adaptation based on experience during my journey.

Discontentment/Precontemplation: You're unhappy about certain aspects of your life. You convince yourself that maybe they aren't horrible, but you know they could be better. In this stage, you may try to repress your discontent and tell yourself things like "It isn't that bad," "It could be worse," and "I can handle it." You deal with life as it is because it's familiar and doesn't require you to fear change.

Breaking Point/Contemplation: Your level of discontent has built to a point that you don't want to tolerate anymore. You have realized that you have a problem and tell yourself things like "I can't do this", "I can't take it anymore" and "I can't go on like this". Usually, you reach the breaking point when triggered by an event that causes you great physical or emotional pain. You start to think a little more seriously about making changes, but may not know where to start.

Decision/Preparation: You decide that you're ready to make a change. You try to figure out what route you want to take to get to where you need to be and feel as though you can see the sun coming up just over the hill.

From here, you could go in a couple of different directions. You can launch yourself forward:

Action: You have determined what route you want to take to reach your destination happiness, and you get started. You release the emergency brake, step on the gas and off you go!

Maintenance: You are sustaining the more healthy behaviors and habits you've established. Resisting temptation becomes easier and you have a more positive outlook. You have more confidence in yourself and God because you see that you have more power over your life than you originally thought.

Or you get stuck in the change roundabout:

Fear: You move from empowered to fearful. The thought of changing makes you anxious. You doubt yourself and your decision to change. You say things like "It's going to be too hard" and "I'm just not strong enough" as well as other limiting beliefs we've already discussed. You begin to feel hopeless and helpless.

Amnesia: As fear grows, you forget why you wanted to change to begin with. Change is now causing you more anxiety than the event that caused your breaking point. You tell yourself things like "It isn't so bad", "I won't let it get out of control again" and other statements you told yourself in the Discomfort/Precontemplation phase. In this stage, you may talk yourself out of trying to change.

When you get stuck in one of these phases, your change cycle turns into your change circle. It loops around over and over and you may continue to be stuck in the roundabout until you figure out what is causing your inability to launch forward and how to straighten the wheel. I've listed a few possible reasons you may get stuck. Which one(s) do you think apply to you?

1. You don't really want to change. You're happy with life as it is.
2. Despite what other people tell you, you don't see the price you pay to Bill.
3. You don't have enough fuel (big enough motivation).
4. You're letting your fear run over you.
5. You don't have enough Faith Power.
6. You're still parking in the middle of the road (not committed to the decision to change).
7. You've not yet released the emergency brake (beliefs that hold you back).
8. You don't trust that God is going to lead you through this.
9. You're attached to addiction.
10. You benefit from the problems addiction causes more than you think you would benefit from change (victim mindset, attention, etc.).

Once you have realized what is holding you back, go back and re-read the chapter(s) and completed worksheet(s) pertaining to that reason.

If you still have difficulties getting out of the roundabout, I will strongly encourage you to pray about those specific reasons. It may also help to get input from someone in your positive friends circle. Often those that have been through their own change cycle can help you to navigate yours.

Hiring a coach might also be an avenue you could take. Coaches are not counselors. The biggest difference is that counseling helps to heal issues from your past and coaching focuses on your future. Coaches are trained to help you figure out where you are stuck and how to move past those areas. Their focus is helping you to steer out of the change cycle roundabout and make it to the finish line. Therapy is very useful in helping you resolve past issues, but as we've discussed, addiction is caused by your current decisions. Whomever you hire, please ensure they are a Christian Coach or Counselor. I have found that their methods and tools are completely different.

You need to believe that you can do this too.

You CAN do this! And I have no doubts that you WILL do this! You need to believe that you can do this too. Remember that you are not alone. Regardless of where you are, our Father created you to grow and mature. He is still in the pace car leading you forward and there are a multitude of people that want to help you through.

> *21 when you heard about Christ and were taught in him in accordance with the truth that is in Jesus. 22 you were taught, with regard to your former way of life, to put off your old self, which is being corrupted by its deceitful desires; 23 to be made new in the attitude of your minds; 24 and to put on the new self, created to be like God in true righteousness and holiness. (Ephesians 4:21-24, NIV)*

The following Reflections page is a great place for you to write your thoughts. You can list areas where you feel you're getting stuck and ideas to steer yourself out of the roundabout.

Reflections

Chapter 13

Avoid Getting Sideswiped by Guilt and Shame

If you're like most people that have decided to give up destructive behaviors, two of the major factors in your breaking point are guilt and shame. I honestly can't remember a day when I didn't feel these emotions in the last 5 years or more of my drunken days. I would be driving down the road and all of a sudden guilt would come out of nowhere and barrel right into the side of me. I would try to regain my composure and keep between the lines just to find shame alongside guilt pushing me into the ditch. It didn't matter what time of day it was or what I was doing, they were always shoving me sideways. Guilt and shame are so heavy.

What happens is, you feel guilt from behaving a certain way, then another layer of guilt for the addiction that causes you to behave in certain ways, and yet another layer for not kicking Bill to the curb sooner. The guilt makes you feel ashamed and now you have so many layers of heaviness pushing you off track that it makes traveling in a straight line seem a lot more difficult than it really is.

Often, when dealing with the primary guilt and shame, you'll have to work backwards and deal with the final layer first. In this case, it's feeling guilt and shame because you haven't kicked Bill to the curb. You're working on that now, right?

You may be asking, "Why shouldn't I feel guilty or ashamed?" A short answer is because guilt and shame are negative emotions. They lead to self-judgment and convince you to believe the worst about yourself. You find yourself measuring your worth by the less than desirable things you've done. This in turn, gives your inner critic a reason to stand up and scream not so

The feelings of guilt and shame give Satan ammunition.

nice stuff. The feelings of guilt and shame give Satan ammunition. They allow him to assign your value and torture you while you're already vulnerable. He may have even already convinced you that you deserve your current hell.

Guilt and shame can also cause you to over catastrophize the events that you feel guilty about. In this case, you feel like whatever it is that you've done is a way bigger problem than it truly is. You may even be the only person that has knowledge of the event and consequences. It's possible for over catastrophizing to create so much fear that it leads you into denial. You don't want to believe that you've done something so horrible and persuade yourself that it never happened. That you don't have a problem. It takes you right back into the amnesia stage in the change cycle.

Remorse on the other hand may seem like a negative emotion, but it has positive effects. It leads to acknowledging that you have made mistakes and taking responsibility for them. This is the emotion that opens your mind, heart and soul to honest apology and repentance.

> *9 If we confess our sins, he is faithful and just and will forgive us our sins and purify us from all unrighteousness. 10 If we claim we have not sinned, we make him out to be a liar and his word is not in us. (1 John 1:9-10, NIV)*

Disappointment is a much healthier emotion than shame. Much like remorse, this emotion allows you to acknowledge and take responsibility for your mistakes. Let's be real for a moment and accept that we all make mistakes. We all have behaviors and habits that we are less than proud of. It's perfectly acceptable to feel disappointment from time to time. When you are able to accept that none other than the Trinity are perfect, you can make adjustments to your attitude and you'll find the desire and motivation to place yourself into the action phase of the change cycle. What you're going through right now might seem terrible, but God's plan for you is good.

> *1 As for you, you were dead in your transgressions and sins, 2 in which you used to live when you followed the ways of this world and of the ruler of the kingdom of the air, the spirit who is now at work in those who are disobedient. 3 All of us also lived among them at one time, gratifying the cravings of our flesh and following its desires and thoughts. Like the rest, we were by nature deserving of wrath. 4 But because of his great love for us, God, who is rich in mercy, 5 made us alive with Christ even when we were dead in transgressions—it is by grace you have been saved. (Ephesians 2:1-5, NIV)*

If you're struggling to stay on the road after being sideswiped by guilt and shame, I get it. It's not always easy to shake off what the devil puts in your head. He likes to hang out where you struggle and is no doubt, doing his best to shove you into the ditch. Think of it this way. Not only have each and every one of us made mistakes, we did so out of ignorance. We were doing what we knew at the time, not realizing we had other options. Now you know that you don't have to struggle anymore. You have the ability to make more appropriate decisions. Now you realize that God loves you regardless of your past and just wants you to lean on Him so He can help you get to your Destination Happiness.

> *20 Even if we feel guilty, God is greater than our feelings, and He knows everything. 21 Dear friends, if we don't feel guilty, we can come to God with bold confidence. (1 John 3:20-21, NLT)*

Use the following Reflections page to write the things you feel the most guilty and shameful about. Also list ideas for kicking the guilt and shame to the curb and things you can do to avoid getting sideswiped by guilt and shame to begin with.

Reflections

Chapter 14

Give Forgiveness a Front Seat

For a long time after I left Bill in the dust, I couldn't shake the guilt and shame I felt for the years of letting it control me. I couldn't figure out why I was having such a hard time getting past it until I realized I had left my forgiveness locked away in the trunk. I was sitting alone one evening, praying for Almighty assistance when I heard the words, "Child, you've got to give forgiveness a front seat! You have it locked away like you're afraid of it."

He had already forgiven me. My past, every mistake I made and every sinful behavior I indulged in were washed away by Jesus' blood centuries ago. Not only have they been forgiven, they have also been forgotten. I am reminded of this every time I read Isaiah.

> *"I—yes, I alone—will blot out your sins for my own sake and will never think of them again. (Isaiah 43:25, NLT)*

The words spoken into my mind that night sparked several days and evenings of deliberation. If the single most important person that ever existed has forgiven me and forgotten every horrible thing I had ever done, who am I to hold a grudge against myself?

One of the things that was happening is that I was having trouble discerning the difference between conviction and condemnation. I was condemning myself with Satan's help. Our Father however, does not condemn. He convicts. He shows us the error in our ways with love and encouragement, leading us to a better path. Conviction creates hope. Condemnation is disapproval of self and spirals out of control very quickly. It is hateful and leads us into darkness. Note the teachings in the following verses.

> *So now there is no condemnation for those who belong to Christ Jesus. (Romans 8:1, NLT)*

> *God sent his Son into the world not to judge the world, but to save the world through Him. (John 3:17, NLT)*

> *I will not judge those who hear me but don't obey me, for I have come to save the world and not to judge it. (John 12:47, NLT)*

While I was writing the last chapter I was praying for you. I asked that while you were working through the feelings of guilt and shame, you were able to find a little forgiveness for yourself. Forgiveness is an extremely important aspect of this journey and the healing process. We tend to punish ourselves and others when we've made a mistake and let's face it, while living in our addiction, we made a lot of mistakes!

Forgiveness is freedom.

Until you accept that mistakes are a part of life and you are already forgiven by God, you may unconsciously sabotage yourself, your progress, and maybe even those around you. Forgiveness is freedom. It has the ability to free you from the limiting beliefs and negative thoughts that weigh on you. It allows us to feel empathy for ourselves and others, freeing us from judgmental beliefs. It provides us with positive emotions and hope.

Forgiving yourself isn't saying that things you've done are okay or denying any wrongdoing. It's acknowledging that you were born an imperfect human you, and you have made mistakes. It's empathizing with the person you believed yourself to be at that time and showing compassion for him/her. It is accepting yourself, understanding yourself and making amends with yourself. It's letting go of the harsh things you allow Satan and your inner critic to convince you of. Then trusting that although you're still going to make mistakes, you're not going to repeat the ones that you now find undesirable. After all, as you've already learned, our Father has given you the power and tools to prevail.

God loves you on your best days and God still loves you on your worst days.

God loves you on your best days and God still loves you on your worst days. As a parent, I don't know if I would have the strength to send my child away to endure the life Jesus lived or to die the death He died. Our Father did though. The sole purpose of Jesus' birth, death and resurrection was our forgiveness. Because of this, Jesus knows what it is like to be you. He understands. You are forgiven. And you are loved.

> *34 Who then is left to condemn us? Certainly not Jesus, the Anointed One! For he gave his life for us, and even more than that, he has conquered death and is now risen, exalted, and enthroned by God at his right hand. So how could he possibly condemn us since he is continually praying for our triumph? 35 Who could ever divorce us from the endless love of God's Anointed One? Absolutely no one! For nothing in the universe has the power to diminish his love toward us. Troubles, pressures, and problems are unable to come between us and heaven's love. What about persecutions, deprivations, dangers, and death threats? No, for they are all impotent to hinder omnipotent love, 36 even though it is written: All day long we face death threats for your sake, God. We are considered to be nothing more than sheep to be slaughtered! 37 Yet even in the midst of all these things, we triumph over them all, for God has made us to be more than conquerors, and his demonstrated love is our glorious victory over everything! 38 So now I live with the confidence that there is nothing in the universe with the power to separate us from God's love. I'm convinced that his love will triumph over death, life's troubles, fallen angels, or dark rulers in the heavens. There is nothing in our present or future circumstances that can weaken his love. 39 There is no power above us or beneath us—no power that could ever be found in the universe that can distance us from God's passionate love, which is lavished upon us through our Lord Jesus, the Anointed One! (Romans 8:34-39, TPT)*

In Colossians, Paul wrote instructions on how to develop some of the characteristics of Jesus. He instructs us to make allowances for the faults of others according to the teachings of Jesus.

> *12 Since God chose you to be the holy people he loves, you must clothe yourselves with tenderhearted mercy, kindness, humility, gentleness, and patience. 13 Make allowance for each other's faults, and forgive anyone who offends you. Remember, the Lord forgave you, so you must forgive others. (Colossians 3:12-13, NLT)*

Notice the words in the center of the last sentence. "the Lord forgave you," followed by "so you must forgive others." This verse reassures you that you have been forgiven and provides the instruction of forgiving those that you feel have contributed to negative aspects of your life.

In this book, we aren't going to spend a lot of time discussing forgiveness of others. I will provide you with a few verses of scripture from The Book, because it is important. In fact, it's disobedient to not forgive others. I believe that right now though, you need to learn to forgive yourself. Forgiving others will be much easier after you have mastered this.

> *31 Get rid of all bitterness, rage, anger, harsh words, and slander, as well as all types of evil behavior. 32 Instead, be kind to each other, tenderhearted, forgiving one another, just as God through Christ has forgiven you. (Ephesians 4:31-32, NLT)*

> *14 If you forgive those who sin against you, your heavenly Father will forgive you. 15 But if you refuse to forgive others, your Father will not forgive your sins. (Matthew 6:14-15, NLT)*

> *And whenever you stand praying, if you find that you carry something in your heart against another person, release him and forgive him so that your Father in heaven will also release you and forgive you of your faults. (Mark 11:25, TPT)*

> ***A poem of insight and instruction by King David***
> *1 What bliss belongs to the one*
> *whose rebellion has been forgiven,*
> *those whose sins are covered by blood.*
> *2 What bliss belongs to those*
> *who have confessed their corruption to God!*
> *For he wipes their slates clean*
> *and removes hypocrisy from their hearts.*
> *3 Before I confessed my sins, I kept it all inside;*
> *my dishonesty devastated my inner life,*
> *causing my life to be filled with frustration,*
> *irrepressible anguish, and misery.*
> *4 The pain never let up, for your hand of conviction*
> *was heavy on my heart.*
> *My strength was sapped, my inner life dried up*
> *like a spiritual drought within my soul.*
> *Pause in his presence*
> *5 Then I finally admitted to you all my sins,*
> *refusing to hide them any longer.*
> *I said, "My life-giving God,*
> *I will openly acknowledge my evil actions."*

> *And you forgave me!*
> *All at once the guilt of my sin washed away*
> *and all my pain disappeared!*
> *Pause in his presence*
> *6 This is what I've learned through it all:*
> *All believers should confess their sins to God;*
> *do it every time God has uncovered you*
> *in the time of exposing.*
> *For if you do this, when sudden storms of life overwhelm,*
> *you'll be kept safe.*
> *7 Lord, you are my secret hiding place,*
> *protecting me from these troubles,*
> *surrounding me with songs of gladness!*
> *Your joyous shouts of rescue release my breakthrough.*
> *Pause in his presence*
> *8-9 I hear the Lord saying, "I will stay close to you,*
> *instructing and guiding you along the pathway for your life.*
> *I will advise you along the way*
> *and lead you forth with my eyes as your guide.*
> *So don't make it difficult; don't be stubborn*
> *when I take you where you've not been before.*
> *Don't make me tug you and pull you along.*
> *Just come with me!"*
> *10 So my conclusion is this:*
> *Many are the sorrows and frustrations*
> *of those who don't come clean with God.*
> *But when you trust in the Lord for forgiveness,*
> *His wraparound love will surround you.*
> *11 So celebrate the goodness of God!*
> *He shows this kindness to everyone who is his.*
> *Go ahead—shout for joy,*
> *all you upright ones who want to please him!*
> *(Psalm 32, TPT)*

Often, people find it difficult to forgive themselves when they are still struggling with issues you have previously learned how to overcome in this book. Let's take a minute to go through a few steps that may be helpful.

First and foremost, receive God's forgiveness and thank Him for his Mercy and Grace.

Forgiveness Worksheet

Forgiveness is key in finding your Destination Happiness. List everything you have not yet forgiven yourself for. Think of things you punish yourself or others for, things you beat yourself up over, things that cause you to feel guilt, anxiety, or pain and things that allow Satan to get your inner critic stirred up. Use additional paper if needed.

1. ______________________________
2. ______________________________
3. ______________________________
4. ______________________________
5. ______________________________
6. ______________________________
7. ______________________________
8. ______________________________
9. ______________________________
10. ______________________________
11. ______________________________
12. ______________________________
13. ______________________________
14. ______________________________
15. ______________________________
16. ______________________________
17. ______________________________
18. ______________________________

On a separate sheet of paper, place each item in the blanks of one of the following sentences.

1. I am forgiving myself for ______________________________ because God already has.

2. I will no longer punish myself for ________________ since God has already forgiven me.

3. I will not listen to negative self-talk about _______________. Jesus has already forgotten.

4. God is no longer concerned with _________________ as it is the past and not my future.

5. I have made mistakes in my past such as ___________________, and Jesus still loves me.

6. I have been forgiven for ____________________________ and it's time to forgive myself.

7. I am forgiving myself for ____ because I recognize that was done when I was under the influence of Bill and I no longer am.

8. I lay down my inability to forgive myself for ____________________________________. God says It is no longer my burden to bear.

After you are finished filling in the blanks, destroy the original list of things you had not forgiven yourself for. Burn it, rip it into shreds, whatever you choose to do to show your mind that you have laid them down, released yourself and let it go.

Chapter 15

Missing Your Exit

It happens to all of us. We're on our way to the place we want to be, following the directions we've been given, our exit is coming up, and we drive right by it. We've gotten distracted, were deep in thought, were detoured by a roadblock or perhaps we didn't see it up ahead. When this has happened to you, did you give up and go back to the place you came from? I'm sure the answer is no. You doubled back and paid more attention to where you needed to turn or you found another route to get you where you were going.

Did you consider yourself a failure for missing your exit or did you chalk it up to the fact that you simply made a mistake? If you thought you were a failure because of this, you're way too hard on yourself! What could be happening, is that you've become attached to that failure and believe it's who you are instead of what it really is. You let it define you. You wouldn't go around shaking hands saying "Hi, I'm Failure. It's nice to meet you." You don't because, just as you aren't addiction, you aren't failure! You're Bob or Suzie or Joe or whatever your name actually is.

We tend to view failure as an attack on who we are. We see it as this horrible dark "thing" that is always hovering over our heads. If you're not failing once in a while, you aren't learning anything. If you've never failed, you haven't tried anything, taken a risk or chased your dreams.

Failure can be a good thing. One way to become more confident is to become more competent and the way to become competent is by learning from your mistakes. If you want to learn, you have to be open to failure. Since you've already failed a time or two, you can now start developing a record of success. Think back to when you were learning to drive a car. When you got behind the wheel for the first time were you a competent driver? Most likely, it took you a few times to get it right. You made mistakes that taught you what not to do as well as what you should be doing. This happened every time you sat in the driver's seat until you were comfortable, confident and competent.

What failure really is, is an opportunity to overcome. One of the greatest lessons you can learn from it is that no matter how many times you fall, you can always get back up. To fail at something means you had the courage to try. That alone makes you a much stronger person than you give yourself credit for.

> *The Lord upholds all who fall and lifts up all who are bowed down. (Psalm 145:14, NIV)*

Finding yourself in a moment of weakness doesn't mean that you are defeated!

Finding yourself in a moment of weakness doesn't mean that you are defeated! Remember that this is just a moment. Moments don't have to last for the rest of your life. Double back or find that alternative route.

Let's look for a minute at some possible reasons you may have missed your exit and see what you can learn from this opportunity. I have included a page at the end of this chapter for you to write your thoughts.

1. Do you still have fear of the unknown? Do you lack confidence in the fact that you can prevail? Are you unsure of your abilities? If the answer to any of these is yes, you are still stuck in the change cycle roundabout. Hey, it happens. It's a vicious circle. Head back to that chapter and try to work your way out.

> *Do not be afraid or discouraged, for the Lord will personally go ahead of you. He will be with you; he will neither fail you nor abandon you." (Deuteronomy 31:8, NLT)*

2. Are you clinging to what you believed to be "good parts" of your life? Previously, you completed worksheets listing the things Bill has cost you and what life will look like once you have moved past your addiction. Put these together and go over them again. Sometimes, we just need to realize that the benefits of a life free from addiction are far greater than what we're leaving behind.

> *So let's not get tired of doing what is good. At just the right time we will reap a harvest of blessing if we don't give up. (Galatians 6:9, NLT)*

3. Do you keep your foot on the brake by asking "What if I fail"? Oh, but what if you succeed? When Satan is telling you that you aren't good at sober life, add the word "yet" to the phrase he is repeating. Say, "I'm not good at this yet" and try again.

> *"I am leaving you with a gift—peace of mind and heart. And the peace I give is a gift the world cannot give. So don't be troubled or afraid." (John 14:27, NLT)*

Now would be a good time to evaluate the steps you have taken. What worked? What didn't work? What could have worked better? What could you have done differently? Where in the process do you want to start again? What should you do next?

Again, Satan likes to hang out in the areas where you struggle so you'll want to get back on track as quickly as possible. Let's discuss a few ways to keep your tires positioned firmly on his head.

1. Avoid contact with people that are addicted and those who are unbelievers. "Peer pressure" is a real thing. It is within these crowds that resisting temptation is the hardest. The only things that grow in the darkness are unpleasant things. If you are striving for happiness and health, you have to stay in the light.

> *Don't team up with those who are unbelievers. How can righteousness be a partner with wickedness? How can light live with darkness? (2 Corinthians 6:14, NLT)*

> *So stop fooling yourselves! Evil companions will corrupt good morals and character. (1 Corinthians 15:33, TPT)*

Just a note here, you only need to avoid "unhealthy" relationships. Never isolate yourself. If you haven't yet surrounded yourself with a Christian community, please do so now. Loneliness can occur very quickly. Solitude can be a real threat to you emotionally and spiritually. Jesus warns us about this in Matthew 12:43-45.

> *43 "When an evil spirit leaves a person, it goes into the desert, seeking rest but finding none. 44 Then it says, 'I will return to the person I came from.' So it returns and finds its former home empty, swept, and in order. 45 Then the spirit finds seven other spirits more evil than itself, and they all enter the person and live there. And so that person is worse off than before. That will be the experience of this evil generation." (Matthew 12:43-45, NLT)*

2. Steer clear of situations where there is any possibility that temptation may be present. If you find yourself in such a situation, try applying the 5 second rule mentioned earlier. 5-4-3-2-MOVE. Change direction, walk (or run) away, get as far from the temptation as possible as quickly as you can.

> *Run from anything that stimulates youthful lusts. Instead, pursue righteous living, faithfulness, love, and peace. Enjoy the companionship of those who call on the Lord with pure hearts. (2 Timothy 2:22, NLT)*

3. Pray, Pray, Pray! Seriously, prayer is powerful! If you have been praying for a while and don't feel like your prayers are answered the way you expect them to be, change your words. Instead of praying that temptation isn't put in front of you, pray for eyes to see it for what it is and the ability to walk away from it with your head held high. Ask for the Holy Spirit to help you. He is who leads us to repentance and guides us back in the right direction. Don't just say the words. Feel them deeply. Have faith that He is listening, and He is going to get you through. Faith power is where you should put your energy right now. Again, the people of faith in your circle can help you with this. After the temptation has passed, say a prayer of gratitude.

> *"Keep watch and pray, so that you will not give in to temptation. For the spirit is willing, but the body is weak!" (Matthew 26:41, NLT)*

4. Remove triggers. As an example, if you have areas where you commonly indulged in Bill, avoid those areas. When you enter a space such as this, your body releases the chemicals to become prepared to take in Bill. It tricks you into thinking that you want or need your poison. If this area is a place that you absolutely must continue to be in, try to change it up a bit. If

it's in your own home, rearrange furniture, decor, etc. This is a fantastic place to scatter the positive affirmations you created in the Accelerate Your Confidence chapter of this book. Deviate from your normal routine and do not ever use Bill here again. This will lessen your brain's association with the space and Bill, making it less of a trigger each time you enter it. This is just one example. Make adjustments for every area and event where you may be tempted.

> *13 Therefore, put on every piece of God's armor so you will be able to resist the enemy in the time of evil. Then after the battle you will still be standing firm. 14 Stand your ground, putting on the belt of truth and the body armor of God's righteousness. 15 For shoes, put on the peace that comes from the Good News so that you will be fully prepared. 16 In addition to all of these, hold up the shield of faith to stop the fiery arrows of the devil. 17 Put on salvation as your helmet, and take the sword of the Spirit, which is the word of God. (Ephesians 6:13-17, NLT)*

> *If you never faced battles, you could never be victorious.*

5. Look at the situation differently. We often view our troubles as hardship. We get stressed out about them and feel fear even when we aren't in the middle of a crisis. This alone weakens our mind and strength. Imagine for a second, the feeling of excitement you feel when you have just finished something that was important to you. Even if you saw it as a hurdle in the beginning, you now see that you were able to conquer the hurdle and the achievement feels nothing less than amazing. You probably wouldn't be as excited about it if you hadn't had to overcome something to get it done. Without trials, there is no real triumph. If you never faced battles, you could never be victorious. Notice what Paul teaches us in this next verse. Suffering produces endurance, endurance produces character and character produces hope. He tells us in 2 Corinthians not to lose heart. Don't give up. He is reminding us that our troubles are just temporary and that we should focus on the unseen eternal hope of Heaven through Jesus.

> *2 Through him we have also obtained access by faith into this grace in which we stand, and we rejoice in hope of the glory of God. 3 Not only that, but we rejoice in our sufferings, knowing that suffering produces endurance, 4 and endurance produces character, and character produces hope, 5 and hope does not put us to shame, because God's love has been poured into our hearts through the Holy Spirit who has been given to us. (Romans 5:2-5, ESV)*

> *16 Therefore we do not lose heart. Though outwardly we are wasting away, yet inwardly we are being renewed day by day. 17 For our light and momentary troubles are achieving for us an eternal glory that far outweighs them all. 18 So we fix our eyes not on what is seen, but on what is unseen, since what is seen is temporary, but what is unseen is eternal. (2 Corinthians 4:16-18, NIV)*

6. Don't pause. Don't take a break. Don't get discouraged. Don't give up. You've put too much time, emotion and effort into this to give up now! We all fail. Not one of us perfect at executing every task every time. Get back into the driver's seat at this very moment, do what you can do to use this as a learning opportunity and trust God to do what only He can do to get you to your destination.

> *For everyone has sinned; we all fall short of God's glorious standard. (Romans 3:23, NLT)*

> *Why am I discouraged? Why is my heart so sad? I will put my hope in God! I will praise him again—my Savior and my God! (Psalm 42:11, NLT)*

7. Once you have reached your destination again, get out of the car. Don't sit there looking in the rear-view mirror. There is a reason the windshield is so much bigger than your mirrors. You no longer belong in what's behind you. Your new life is in front of you. You can no longer claim to be addicted. You have been made clean by the powers above.

I have known many formerly addicted people that live in constant fear of relapse, tying themselves to an addicted mindset. They put so much energy into the fact that they used to be addicted that they don't realize that they no longer are. They aren't using anymore, but Bill is still controlling them. They haven't fully taken back the wheel and fear they will allow Satan to sabotage them more than they trust God to lead them. Living in fear will never allow you to enjoy the life God has planned for you. You may see the exit to Destination Happiness, but you won't be able to use the ramp to get there.

One phrase I have heard many times is, "once an addict, forever (or always) an addict." Unfortunately, there are several recovery programs that teach this. I wanted to elaborate on this subject just in case you have had this limiting belief programmed into your mind. The groups that hold this view aren't necessarily Christian programs. They do not understand that our Father can and will change you. They rely solely on willpower and abstinence instead of relying on Faithpower, God, and the promises He has made to us.

If you have followed the guidance in this book, you are no longer using Bill, and you have allowed God to change your heart. You no longer desire Bill and no longer put Bill ahead of Him. This is sobriety. This means you are no longer addicted and can no longer consider yourself an addict.

I, in no way, think it's in your best interest to use even a tiny amount of Bill. This could open doors that you have already closed. You've closed the door on your addiction and slammed the door on Satan. Opening it back up again could allow him to slither back in. Keep in mind that snakes can sneak in through very small gaps.

> *25 Look straight ahead, and fix your eyes on what lies before you. 26 Mark out a straight path for your feet; stay on the safe path. 27 Don't get sidetracked; keep your feet from following evil. (Proverbs 4:25-27, NLT)*

> *You make known to me the path of life; in your presence there is fullness of joy; at your right hand are pleasures forevermore. (Psalm 16:11, ESV)*

> *The hopes of the godly result in happiness, but the expectations of the wicked come to nothing. (Proverbs 10:28, NLT)*

Use the following reflections page to work through any issues that are causing you to hit red lights on your journey. Go back through the chapter that deals with those issues until you have resolved them then roll on through the green light.

Reflections

Chapter 16

Celebrate Your Arrival

Congratulations! You made it! Today is the day that life begins! By now you've realized that when you have God in the pace car, Satan doesn't have the power to get ahead of you. I am so excited for you! You should be excited to!

> *Blessed is the one who perseveres under trial because, having stood the test, that person will receive the crown of life that the Lord has promised to those who love him. (James 1:12, NIV)*

Have you noticed that while you were traveling this road to your Destination Happiness your behaviors changed? You are now making decisions that are more healthy for you and those close to you. You have built relationships with people that want to see you succeed in life. You have lost your addiction and gained a closer relationship with our Father. Amen! I knew this day would come!

It's time to celebrate! Not simply celebrate your victory over addiction, celebrate that your heart and spirit are more aligned with God's plan than they previously were. Celebrate your ability to put more faith in Him. Celebrate your freedom. Celebrate all of the blessings that have been, are and will be bestowed upon you. Celebrate your future.

> *All who are victorious will be clothed in white. I will never erase their names from the Book of Life, but I will announce before my Father and his angels that they are Mine. (Revelation 3:5, NLT)*

> *3 Blessed be the God and Father of our Lord Jesus Christ, who has blessed us in Christ with every spiritual blessing in the heavenly places, 4 even as he chose us in him before the foundation of the world, that we should be holy and blameless before him. In love 5 he predestined us for adoption to himself as sons through Jesus Christ, according to the purpose of his will, 6 to the praise of his glorious grace, with which he has blessed us in the Beloved. 7 In him we have redemption through his blood, the forgiveness of our trespasses, according to the riches of his grace, 8 which he lavished upon us, in all wisdom and insight 9 making known to us the mystery of his will, according to his purpose, which he set forth in Christ 10 as a plan for the fullness of time, to unite all things in him, things in heaven and things on earth. 11 In him we have obtained an inheritance, having been predestined according to the purpose of him who works all things according to the counsel of his will, 12 so that we who were the first to hope in Christ might be to the praise of his glory. 13 In him you also, when you heard the word of truth, the gospel of your salvation, and believed in him, were sealed with the promised Holy Spirit, 14 who is the guarantee of our inheritance until we acquire possession of it, to the praise of his lory. (Ephesians 1:3-14, ESV)*

While you're celebrating, don't forget to celebrate that you are forgiven.

> *12 I am writing to you who are God's children because your sins have been forgiven through Jesus. 13 I am writing to you who are mature in the faith because you know Christ, who existed from the beginning. I am writing to you who are young in the faith because you have won your battle with the evil one. 14 I have written to you who are God's children because you know the Father. I have written to you who are mature in the faith because you know Christ, who existed from the beginning. I have written to you who are young in the faith because you are strong. God's word lives in your hearts, and you have won your battle with the evil one. (1 John 2:12-14, NLT)*

Celebrate that as He promised, God stayed with you, guiding your path along the way. He provided you with love, grace, mercy and instructions with every mile you have driven and every obstacle you faced. You have never been, nor will you ever be alone.

> *But by the grace of God I am what I am, and his grace to me was not without effect. No, I worked harder than all of them—yet not I, but the grace of God that was with me. (1 Corinthians 15:10, NIV)*

I hope you celebrated every little accomplishment along the way in this journey. Celebrating milestones helps us to stay motivated and allows us to feel genuine gratitude. Since it's such an effective tool, you don't want to stop the celebration now. Keep rewarding yourself for this achievement, over and over again, as long as you are maintaining your addiction free life. After all, we reward other people for positive behavior, why shouldn't we reward ourselves?

So, what does celebration look like to you? For some, it may be a vacation in the Bahamas while to others it looks more like an expensive cup of java from their favorite coffee shop or a new pair of shoes. Perhaps it's quiet time with a good book or watching an action movie starring your favorite actor. Or maybe a romantic weekend trip with your spouse.

On the next worksheet, list little ways you can reward yourself each day for continuing a life free from addictions. You'll want to come up with several little rewards since they may become so much a part of your routine that they no longer seem to be a reward. Then list bigger ways to celebrate milestones. As an example, after 6 months, one year, etc. At each 5-year mark, celebrate by choosing a "bucket list" reward. Put some of the money you're saving by not paying Bill back to spend for the bigger rewards. You can adjust your lists every time you think of something new or greater.

It is very important that your rewards have nothing to do with your previous addiction, won't remind you of Bill, and won't become a new addiction.

Just a note here that I'm sure you're already aware of but I would be remiss to not mention. It is very important that your rewards have nothing to do with your previous addiction, won't remind you of Bill, and won't become a new addiction. If your Bill was food, you should not reward yourself with dining out, if it was alcohol, don't have a drink, if it was TV, don't sit down to watch a movie. You get what I'm saying. Choose your rewards carefully. Then remember to consistently reward yourself! Again, congratulations! I knew you could do it! I knew the Holy Spirit was within you!

We're not finished yet though. Keep reading.

Celebrating My Arrival Worksheet

What are ways I can reward myself for an addiction free day?

1. ____
2. ____
3. ____
4. ____
5. ____
6. ____
7. ____
8. ____
9. ____
10. ____
11. ____
12. ____
13. ____
14. ____
15. ____

What are ways I can reward myself for an addiction free week or month?

1. ____
2. ____
3. ____

4. ______________________________

5. ______________________________

6. ______________________________

7. ______________________________

8. ______________________________

9. ______________________________

10. ______________________________

11. ______________________________

12. ______________________________

13. ______________________________

14. ______________________________

15. ______________________________

What are ways I can reward myself for remaining addiction free for 3 months, 6 months, etc.?

1. ______________________________

2. ______________________________

3. ______________________________

4. ______________________________

5. ______________________________

6. ______________________________

7. ______________________________

8. ______________________________

9. ______________________________

10. ____

11. ____

12. ____

13. ____

14. ____

15. ____

What are some things that I absolutely want to experience in life that I can do to celebrate every 5 years that I live without Bill?

1. ____

2. ____

3. ____

4. ____

5. ____

6. ____

7. ____

8. ____

9. ____

10. ____

11. ____

12. ____

13. ____

14. ____

Chapter 17

Helping Others Reach Their Destination Happiness

You have arrived at your Destination Happiness, but your journey is not yet finished. As long as you have breath in your lungs you will have purpose. God's plan for you will continuously move you forward towards a new destination.

Don't be afraid of these new adventures. This journey will be more rewarding than I can possibly describe. This is quite an opportunity and an immense honor. This is where life gets really good! Are you excited yet? You should be!

Imagine for a minute, feeling deep love for people, satisfaction with life and true joy. Imagine laying your head on your pillow at night and your sorrows have been replaced with a heart overflowing with fulfillment. I can tell you from my own personal experience that this is what it's like when you go to bed loving Jesus and knowing that you made a difference in someone else's life.

This is your purpose too. It has been all along. Helping others reach their Destination Happiness. So many people are living in the same hell you and God just drove you away from. They have the same fears, thoughts and "buts" you did when you started this journey. They need to see that an addiction free life is not only possible, but also achievable. Who better to help them through than the "one" in the Parable of the Lost Lamb which is now one of the "99"?

> *4-5 "There once was a shepherd with a hundred lambs, but one of his lambs wandered away and was lost. So the shepherd left the ninety-nine lambs out in the open field and searched in the wilderness for that one lost lamb. He didn't stop until he finally found it. With exuberant joy, he raised it up, placed it on his shoulders, and carried it back with cheerful delight! 6 Returning home, he called all his friends and neighbors together and said, 'Let's have a party! Come and celebrate with me the return of my lost lamb. It wandered away, but I found it and brought it home.' " 7 Jesus continued, "In the same way, there will be a glorious celebration in heaven over the rescue of one lost sinner who repents, comes back home, and returns to the old—more so than for all the righteous people who never strayed away." (Luke 15:4-7, TPT)*

Just as I facilitate meetings, coach and have shared this writing to fulfill my purpose, now is the time to help those around you by letting them see what Jesus has done for you, and in you. Just as I have been a tool God provided you with, you are now a tool for others.

> *So now put into practice what I have done for you, and you will experience a life of happiness enriched with untold blessings!" (John 13:17, TPT)*

I spent a great deal of time being too embarrassed to share my story with anyone. It was my little secret. But when our Father speaks, I tend to listen. I might argue a little, but ultimately, I obey. Honestly, I was comfortable in my new life after alcoholism. Until I began serving God by helping those that shared similar stories. Working in my purpose has taken my life to a whole different level. I'm no longer just content. I'm overjoyed. God is using someone as insignificant as me to reach so many of our brothers and sisters. I now realize that my story isn't a description of an alcoholic. It's a narrative of recovery, healing, blessings, mercy, grace and the love of God. I'm excited to tell my story now. Just the thought of it creating an "aha moment" for someone else makes my heart smile.

One of the main things scripture teaches us is that we are to love each other. Every commandment and every lesson instructs us in ways to love and show love. Although there are many ways to express love, the greatest is showing them how to walk closer to our Father and helping them through life's struggles.

> *14 What good is it, my brothers and sisters, if someone claims to have faith but has no deeds? Can such faith save them? 15 Suppose a brother or a sister is without clothes and daily food. 16 If one of you says to them, "Go in peace; keep warm and well fed," but does nothing about their physical needs, what good is it? 17 In the same way, faith by itself, if it is not accompanied by action, is dead. (James 2:14-17, NIV)*

Am I telling you that you have to write a book or become a life coach? No. The gifts that God gave you may differ from mine. We were all created uniquely, with our own talents and abilities. You will work on finding yours in a little while.

> *So we are convinced that every detail of our lives is continually woven together for good, for we are his lovers who have been called to fulfill his designed purpose. (Romans 8:28, TPT)*

One of the greatest things every one of us can do for each other is pray. It's okay if you aren't comfortable praying over people out loud. You can still pray earnestly for them when you are alone. You may not realize this, but you had several people praying for you all throughout your journey. It's time to pray it forward.

It's time to pray it forward.

> *13 Are any of you suffering hardships? You should pray. Are any of you happy? You should sing praises. 14 Are any of you sick? You should call for the elders of the church to come and pray over you, anointing you with oil in the name of the Lord. 15 Such a prayer offered in faith will heal the sick, and the Lord will make you well. And if you have committed any sins, you will be forgiven. 16 Confess your sins to each other and pray for each other so that you may be healed. The earnest prayer of a righteous person has great power and produces wonderful results. (James 5:13-16, NLT)*

> *19 My dear brothers and sisters, if someone among you wanders away from the truth and is brought back, 20 you can be sure that whoever brings the sinner back from wandering will save that person from death and bring about the forgiveness of many sins. (James 5:19-20, NLT)*

I remember a time when I thought I was alone in life. Some would say that I was stubbornly independent, and truth be told, I was. I thought I had to figure it out all on my own and didn't trust anyone to help. I honestly believed that it wasn't possible for anyone other than me to figure out what was needed to make my life better, my decisions wiser or me happier. I'm glad I got over that! Whew! That was a rough period in my life! At that time, I wasn't reading the bible and knew very few verses of scripture. I was ignorant. Ignorant to the fact that there was a better way. Ignorant to the fact that I had options. Ignorant to the fact that our Father knew who I was and loved me anyway. Ignorant to the fact that He was patiently waiting for me to ask Him to release me from Bill. And ignorant to the fact that there were so many other people that had similar experiences as me and were willing to jump in my car and help me stay in the right lane.

I'm sure at some point, you felt this way too. Didn't it inspire so much hope and make the road so much easier to travel when you realized you are not alone? It's up to you now to help other people with this same realization, to be an inspiration and to ensure that they are not alone in their journey.

> *9 Two people are better off than one, for they can help each other succeed. 10 If one person falls, the other can reach out and help. But someone who falls alone is in real trouble. 11 Likewise, two people lying close together can keep each other warm. But how can one be warm alone? 12 A person standing alone can be attacked and defeated, but two can stand back-to-back and conquer. Three are even better, for a triple-braided cord is not easily broken. (Ecclesiastes 4:9-12, NLT)*

Some people spend their entire lifetime trying to figure out what their purpose in life is. I've heard it referred to as "The big question." Often, dwelling on this question causes depression, feelings of worthlessness, and confusion when the person asking doesn't know the answer. I'm so happy you now know what you were created to do. This answers the question of "why did this happen to me" too. We have to have experiences to learn. Even Jesus endured horrible things throughout His time on earth to gain understanding.

> *For we are his workmanship, created in Christ Jesus for good works, which God prepared beforehand, that we should walk in them. (Ephesians 2:10, ESV)*

Psalms 91 serves as a good reminder of what God is willing to do for us because of his unconditional love. It's one of my favorites to share with those that are struggling because sometimes we just need to be reminded.

1 Those who live in the shelter of the Most High
will find rest in the shadow of the Almighty.
2 This I declare about the Lord:
He alone is my refuge, my place of safety;
he is my God, and I trust him.
3 For he will rescue you from every trap
and protect you from deadly disease.
4 He will cover you with his feathers.
He will shelter you with his wings.
His faithful promises are your armor and protection.
5 Do not be afraid of the terrors of the night,
nor the arrow that flies in the day.
6 Do not dread the disease that stalks in darkness,
nor the disaster that strikes at midday.
7 Though a thousand fall at your side,
though ten thousand are dying around you,
these evils will not touch you.
8 Just open your eyes,
and see how the wicked are punished.
9 If you make the Lord your refuge,
if you make the Most High your shelter,
10 no evil will conquer you;
no plague will come near your home.
11 For he will order his angels
to protect you wherever you go.
12 They will hold you up with their hands
so you won't even hurt your foot on a stone.
13 You will trample upon lions and cobras;
you will crush fierce lions and serpents under your feet!
14 The Lord says, "I will rescue those who love me.
I will protect those who trust in my name.
15 When they call on me, I will answer;
I will be with them in trouble.
I will rescue and honor them.
16 I will reward them with a long life
and give them my salvation."
(Psalm 91, NLT)

Here's another thing to be grateful for. This will be the last worksheet for you to complete in this book. Hallelujah! On the following pages, you're going to explore some thoughts about using your experience to help others reach their Destination Happiness. If you have trouble coming up with answers, seek input from your trusted circle, your coach, pastor or groups you have participated in along the way.

I cannot wait until the world gets to see you completely free from addiction, totally free from self-sabotaging behaviors and entirely free from destructive thoughts. I can't wait until the world sees you living your best life!

> *18 I am convinced that any suffering we endure is less than nothing compared to the magnitude of glory that is about to be unveiled within us. 19 The entire universe is standing on tiptoe, yearning to see the unveiling of God's glorious sons and daughters! 20 For against its will the universe itself has had to endure the empty futility resulting from the consequences of human sin. But now, with eager expectation, 21 all creation longs for freedom from its slavery to decay and to experience with us the wonderful freedom coming to God's children. (Romans 8:18-21, TPT)*

Helping Others Reach Their Destination Happiness Worksheet

What did God teach me about Himself during my addiction?

1.____

2.____

3.____

4.____

5.____

6.____

7.____

8.____

9.____

10. _______________________________________

What did God teach me about Himself during my recovery?

1.____

2.____

3.____

4.____

5.____

6.____

7.____

8.____

9.____

10. ____

What did God teach me about myself during my recovery?

1.____

2.____

3.____

4.____

5.____

6.____

7.____

8.____

9.____

10. ____

Where do I see God giving me opportunities to use my story of addiction and recovery to encourage and help others?

1.____

2.____

3.____

4.____

5.____

6.____

7.____

8.____

9.____

10. ____

What are some things I can do to support others in their recovery journey?

1.____

2.____

3.____

4.____

5.____

6.____

7.____

8.____

9.____

10. ____

You, my friend, are amazing. I'm absolutely ecstatic that I was able to accompany you on your journey to your Destination Happiness. I want to remind you that even though you have arrived, you are still not alone. I will be with you in your thoughts as long as you allow me to be there and you will be in my prayers always. We are both so very fortunate to have Jesus in the middle, holding our hands. For now, I leave you with this:

God's Constant Love

1 Let everyone give all their praise and thanks to the Lord!
Here's why—he's better than anyone could ever imagine.
Yes, he's always loving and kind, and his faithful love never ends.
2-3 So, go ahead—let everyone know it!
Tell the world how he broke through
and delivered you from the power of darkness and
has gathered us together from all over the world.
He has set us free to be his very own!
4 Some of us once wandered in the wilderness like desert nomads,
with no true direction or dwelling place.
5 Starving, thirsting, staggering,
we became desperate and filled with despair.
6 Then we cried out, "Lord, help us! Rescue us!" And he did!
7 He led us out by the right way
until we reached a suitable city to dwell in.
8 So lift your hands and thank God for his marvelous kindness
and for all his miracles of mercy for those he loves.
9 How he satisfies the souls of thirsty ones
and fills the hungry with goodness!
10 Some of us once sat in darkness,
living in the dark shadows of death.
We were prisoners to our pain, chained to our regrets.
11 For we rebelled against God's Word
and rejected the wise counsel of God Most High.
12 So he humbled us through our circumstances,
watching us as we stumbled, with no one there to pick us back up.
Our own pain became our punishment.
13 Then we cried out, "Lord, help us! Rescue us!" And he did!
14 His light broke through the darkness and
he led us out in freedom from death's dark shadow
and snapped every one of our chains.
15 So lift your hands and give thanks to God for his marvelous kindness

and for his miracles of mercy for those he loves!
16 For he smashed through heavy prison doors and
shattered the steel bars that held us back, just to set us free!
17 Some of us were such fools, bringing on ourselves
sorrow and suffering all because of our sins.
18 Sick and feeble, unable to stand the sight of food,
we drew near to the gates of death.
19 Then we cried out, "Lord, help us! Rescue us!" And he did!
20 God spoke the words "Be healed," and we were healed,
delivered from death's door!
21 So lift your hands and give thanks to God for his marvelous kindness
and for his miracles of mercy for those he loves!
22 Bring your praise as an offering and your thanks as a sacrifice
as you sing your story of miracles with a joyful song.
23 Some of us set sail upon the sea to faraway ports,
transporting our goods from ship to shore.
24 We were witnesses of God's power out in the ocean deep;
we saw breathtaking wonders upon the high seas.
25 When God spoke he stirred up a storm,
lifting high the waves with hurricane winds.
26-27 Ships were tossed by the swelling sea, rising to the sky,
then dropping down to the depths,
reeling like drunkards, spinning like tops,
everyone at their wits' end until even sailors despaired of life, cringing in terror.
28 Then we cried out, "Lord, help us! Rescue us!" And he did!
29 God stilled the storm, calmed the waves,
and he hushed the hurricane winds to only a whisper.
30 We were so relieved, so glad as he guided us
safely to harbor in a quiet haven.
31 So lift your hands and give thanks to God for his marvelous kindness
and for his miracles of mercy for those he loves!
32 Let's exalt him on high and lift up our praises in public;
let all the people and the leaders of the nation know

> *how great and wonderful is Yahweh, our God!*
> *33 Whenever he chooses he can dry up a river*
> *and turn the land into a desert.*
> *34 Or he can take a fruitful land and make it into a saltwater swamp,*
> *all because of the wickedness of those who dwell there.*
> *35 But he also can turn a barren wilderness into an oasis with water!*
> *He can make springs flow into desert lands*
> *36 and turn them into fertile valleys so that cities spring up,*
> *and he gives it all to those who are hungry.*
> *37 They can plant their fields and vineyards there*
> *and reap a bumper crop and gather a fruitful harvest.*
> *38 God will bless them and cause them to multiply and prosper.*
> *39 But others will become poor,*
> *humbled because of their oppression, tyranny, and sorrows.*
> *40 For God pours contempt upon their arrogant abuse of power,*
> *heaping scorn upon their princes,*
> *and makes them wander among ruins.*
> *41 But he raises up the poor and lowly with his favor,*
> *giving them a safe place to live where no one can touch them.*
> *God will grant them a large family and bless them!*
> *42 The lovers of God will rejoice when they see this.*
> *Good men are glad when the evil ones are silenced.*
> *43 If you are truly wise, you'll learn from what I've told you.*
> *It's time for you to consider these profound lessons*
> *of God's great love and mercy!*
> *(Psalm 107, TPT)*

Reflections

About the Author

Lissa Patterson is an Author of Christian Self-Help and other Christian Life Coaching articles. After over 20 years living the addicted life, she allowed God to take control and is completely free from alcoholism and cigarettes. She is now an Ordained Minister with a focus on Life Coach Ministry as well as the owner of Metanoia Life Recovery Coaching. She believes overcoming addictions and relinquishing destructive behaviors can be achieved without relying on willpower or your own ability when you let God take the lead.

She is passionate about helping others grow through life's toughest battles and serving God. When she isn't telling others about Jesus, you'll find her with a good book in hand, increasing her knowledge, writing, caring for her multiple houseplants or enjoying the company of her family in the breathtaking Missouri Ozarks. Early in the morning when the sun is rising and the birds are singing; you'll find her sharing time with Jesus while outside with her Bible and a cup of coffee.

www.ingramcontent.com/pod-product-compliance
Lightning Source LLC
LaVergne TN
LVHW080847170826
845678LV00006B/1740

9798995626602